Six Sigma Simplified

Breakthrough Improvement Made Easy

3rd Edition

Six Sigma® Simplified – Breakthrough Improvement Made Easy 3rd Edition
© 2004 by Jay Arthur

Published by LifeStar
2244 S. Olive St.
Denver, CO 80224-2518
(888) 468-1535 or (303) 757-2039 (orders only)
(888) 468-1537 or (303) 756-9144 (phone)
(888) 468-1536 or (303) 756-3107 (fax)
lifestar@rmi.net
www.qimacros.com
www.sixsigmatoolbelt.com

Upgrade Your KnowWare®!

ISBN 1-884180-13-2

Any Six Sigma Simplified book can be customized to reflect a company's improvement process. For information, call, write, or e-mail to the address above.

Also by Jay Arthur:
The Six Sigma Instructor's Guide, Greenbelt Training Made Easy, LifeStar, 2003
The Small Business Guerrilla Guide to Six Sigma, LifeStar, 2003.
The Six Sigma Tools Example Book, LifeStar, 2003.

Phone, Fax, or E-mail support: Contact Jay Arthur at the phone, fax or e-mail address above for any questions you have about Six Sigma Improvement or using this book.

 **Jay Arthur,** The KnowWare® Man, works with companies that want to systematically plug the leaks in their cash flow. Jay specializes in transactional (i.e., orders, billing, purchasing, payments, claims, etc.) or IT-based Six Sigma improvements. He has helped large companies save millions of dollars and small companies cut costs and boost profits.

Six Sigma is a registered trade and service mark of Motorola, Inc.

Table of Contents

Six Sigma Simplified

This Six Sigma Simplified Workbook is designed to make learning the principles and processes of Six Sigma more easy. The fill-in-the-blanks simplicity of this book makes it easy for anyone to learn the fundamental tools of Six Sigma and the step-by-step way to employ them for maximum benefit.

Robin Hood

1. If you don't know anything about Six Sigma or the improvement processes, read the Improvement Story on our website: www.sixsigmatoolbelt.com/pdf/sixsigmastory.pdf.

Six Sigma

2. If you know something about Six Sigma or quality improvement, then consider starting at the section on Making Six Sigma Pay Off. There are lots of ways to implement improvement projects; most are doomed to failure if you don't understand the science behind the implementation of change.

Breakthrough Improvement

DMAIC

3. The rest of the book covers how to:
   - **Implement Six Sigma Successfully.** Getting into Six Sigma can be either a huge expense or cost effective. The difference is in how it's implemented.
   - **Focus your improvements (i.e., Define and Measure)** like a laser to maximize benefits and minimize costs.
   - **Analyze and Improve key processes** to make them better, faster, and cheaper.
     - Double your speed by eliminating delay
     - Double your quality by preventing defects
   - **Sustain the improvements (i.e., Control)** to ensure you don't slide back.
   - **Honor your progress** to recognize and reward the pioneering efforts of your employees.

4. There are four key elements of Six Sigma:
   - **Root-Cause Analysis** to reduce or eliminate *defects*
   - **Value-Added Analysis** to reduce or eliminate *delays*

SPC
   - **Statistical Process Control (SPC)** to monitor and sustain the new levels of performance.

DFSS
   - **Design for Six Sigma (DFSS)** to create <u>new products or services</u>, and the processes for delivering them, that will start at 4.5 sigma (1,000 PPM) vs 2-sigma for most new products.

Turn Your Cash Cow Into A Golden Goose

Why Six Sigma?

I spent 21 years working in various parts of the Bell System—one of the best cash cows of the last century. In the 1990s I lead teams that, in a matter of months, saved $20 million in postage expense and $16 million in adjustment costs.

Other teams reduced computer downtime by 74% in just six months. Since then, I've helped other companies find ways to save $250,000 per project or more. And you can too, using the power of Six Sigma.

Has your business grown into a cash cow? Are you comfortable with your current level of productivity and profitability? Or do you still have a nagging feeling that they could be much higher? Well they can be and here's why:

Unwanted Side Effects

Plug the Leaks in Your Cash Flow

I have found that every business process produces two unwanted side-effects: *defects* and *delay*. These can be reduced or eliminated completely with Six Sigma which will **save 25-35% of ongoing costs.**

Primitive Tools and Archaic Methods

Virtually all companies grow from wobbly start-ups into a cash cows using trial-and-error and common sense. But most companies stop improving when they reach 1%, 2%, or 3% error levels (3-Sigma) in marketing, sales, ordering, and billing.

The primitive methods and tools that took you to sustainable profitability will take you no farther.

Benefits of Six Sigma

To turn your Cash Cow into a Golden Goose you will need the common science of Six Sigma to rise to 5-Sigma and beyond. Here's what you can accomplish with Six Sigma:

1. Double your speed without working harder. Most companies have extensive delays *built into* their processes.

2. Double your quality by reducing defects 50% or more.

3. Cut costs and boost profits because every dollar you used to spend fixing problems can now be refocused on growing the business or passed right through to the bottom line.

A Tale of Two Factories

The Fix-it Factory

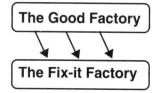

Every company has two "factories:"

♦ the "Good" Factory that creates and delivers your product or service

♦ and a hidden "Fix-it" factory that cleans up all of the mistakes and delays that occur in the main factory.

If your company is a 3-Sigma company (and most companies are), then the Fix-it Factory is costing you $25-40 of every $100 you spend.

Expenses	Potential Savings
$1 million	$250,000-400,000
$10 million	$2.5-4 million
$100 million	$25-40 million
$1 billion	$250-400 million

Just think what saving a fraction of that waste could do for your productivity and profitability!

The End of Common Sense

We know that there are wave lengths of light that we cannot see with our eyes. And low pitched and high pitched sounds that only our dogs can hear. The same is true in business, there are levels of defects that we can't detect. This level is around 1-3% defects or 3 Sigma.

When I worked in the phone company, managers used to say "Well it's just common sense," but what I've learned is that common sense will only get you to a 3% defect rate. Most hospitals get to a 1% error rate on things like infection rates and medication errors, but that's where they reach the edges of human perception, *the end of common sense.*

Doctors routinely use diagnostic tools like EKGs, X-Rays, and MRIs to detect possible problems in the body. Shouldn't we use a more advanced set of tools to diagnose problems in the corporate body?

When you reach the end of what you can do with one problem solving technology (e.g., common sense), you need to look to the next level: systematic problem solving and the tools of Six Sigma.

Jumping The Curve

In *The Structure of Scientific Revolutions*, Thomas Kuhn found that humans are natural problem solvers. He discovered a pattern to our ongoing ability to solve problems: an S curve. When confronted with a new type of problem, new solutions are tried and the most successful one is rapidly adopted. But over time, the solution's ability to solve that class of problems levels off (e.g., antibiotics fight bacterial infections, but not viral ones).

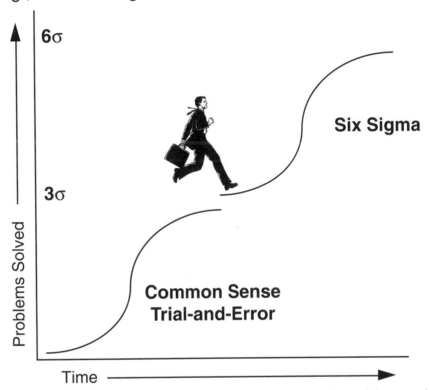

At this point, almost everyone is fully vested in the old paradigm and a fringe group is exploring ways to "jump the curve" to the next paradigm of solution. The success of the old solution often blinds people to the value of a new solution (e.g., digital vs the mainspring watch, cell phone vs wired phone).

I find the same thing holds true when working with managers and business owners. The instinctive methods of solving problems level off at about 3-sigma.

If you want to move to higher levels of quality and profitability, you're going to want to jump the curve by learning to apply the enhanced methods and tools of Six Sigma Simplified.

Manufacturing vs Service

The End of Manufacturing

I can't tell you how many times I've heard people say: "Six Sigma...isn't that just for manufacturing?" The short answer is: No, Six Sigma is good for ANY business process—information technology, customer service, administrative, whatever.

Why? Because **every business suffers from the two key problems that Six Sigma can solve: defects and delay.**

If you look closely at American industry, more and more manufacturing jobs are moving offshore. More than half of the gross national product comes from information and service industries like Microsoft and McDonalds. But these industries are lagging behind manufacturing in the quest for quality.

That's why there's so much opportunity for the business that decides to use Six Sigma to breakthrough to new levels of productivity and profitability—no one else is doing it!

When I first started working with Total Quality Management (TQM) in the phone company, many people said it wouldn't work because TQM only works for manufacturing, not services. Nothing could be further from the truth. This is just a convenient way for crafty employees to dodge learning these powerful improvement strategies.

What is Manufacturing?

Those activities relating to the development and production of tangible products. Other terms used to describe these are "plant floor," "production," "engineering" or "product development." Driven by the marketplace, most manufacturing functions have had to embrace improvement methodologies and statistical process control (SPC) just to survive.

What are Services?

According to Peter Pande, the answer is: sales, finance, marketing, procurement, customer support, logistics, IT, or HR. A few of the other words used to describe these activities include: transactional, commercial, nontechnical, support, and administration. These business functions have tried to hide from Six Sigma and many have been successful, but the wisdom of Six Sigma is shifting from blue-collar jobs to white-collar ones.

Manufacturing vs Service

At an abstract level there's no real difference between a service process and a manufacturing one. They both encounter delays, defects, and costs. One may produce purchase orders instead of computers, bills instead of brake liners, but they all take time, cost money, create defects, cause rework, and create waste.

IT

In an IT department, we might focus on downtime or transaction delays. We might focus on manual rework of order errors or the costs of fixing billing errors. Even a great manufacturing company can suffer tremendously from IT problems.

Healthcare

In a hospital, we might focus on medication errors. We might focus on admission, diagnosis, treatment, or discharge delays. We might focus on the costs of medical errors that result in longer hospital stays.

Finance

In a hospital, the clinical side is only one element. Defects and delays in issuing bills and insurance claims can cost millions of dollars. This is true in any company from a family-owned restaurant to a Fortune 500 company. Incorrect bills, missing charges, incorrect purchase orders, overpayment, underpayment, and so on can cost a fortune. Fielding the phone calls and fixing the financial transaction can cost more than some invoices are worth.

Purchasing

Purchasing is another area for investigation. What does it cost to get quotes from three different vendors for the same product? What does it cost when you delay a purchase to squeeze a couple of extra pennies off the order? What does it cost when you order the wrong part and it stops your production line?

Customer Service

What does it cost to take a call from a customer? The average is around $9. Are your systems and literature setup to force your customer to call you for every little thing? Or are your systems set up to let the customer serve themselves when they need it?

So, if you're a good manufacturing company, use Six Sigma to simplify and streamline your "service" components.

If you're a good service company, use Six Sigma to make breakthrough improvements that will differentiate you from all of your competitors.

Small Business & Six Sigma

Are you a Six Sigma Guerrilla? Are you willing to ignore the prevailing, but incorrect "wisdom" about how to implement a systematic improvement methodology like Six Sigma? Are you willing to start making immediate improvements in productivity and profitability *using only a small fraction of your employees, time, and money*? Or would you rather spend a lot of time and money and then have to wait up to a year for bottom-line, profit-enhancing results?

Bypassing the BS

If you've been reading about Six Sigma and you are wondering how you can get the big benefits without all of the expense, then this book is for you. A 2003 study by Quality Digest magazine confirmed what I've known for years: *a handful of tools and methods are delivering most of the benefit of Six Sigma.* Focused application of these tools will carry you from average to excellent (3-sigma to 5-sigma) in as little as 18-24 months, *while delivering staggering improvements in productivity and profits.*

Don't Let the Name Fool You

Six Sigma...even the name sounds complex doesn't it? But it doesn't have to be. This book will cover the bare-bones, essential methods and tools you need to know to start making breakthrough improvements. Like most things in life, 20% of the methods and tools will give you 80% of the benefit. These are the tools I use day in and day out with clients and in my business to make quantum leaps in performance. You can too.

Get in Cheap!

You can spend $15,000 training one Six Sigma Blackbelt and an estimated $250,000 total before they are fully effective, but the methods in this book will carry you from 3-to-5 sigma without spending all that time and cash.

In God We Trust, All Others Must Bring Data

The March 2003 issue of Quality Digest Magazine explored the results of their Six Sigma Survey. What did they discover?

Small Business & Six Sigma

1. Small companies aren't pursuing Six Sigma. Why not? It costs too much and takes too long using the traditional Six Sigma approach.

2. Companies pursuing Six Sigma seem to abandon it after two or three years. Why? One reason might be that the average life-span of a CEO is only 2-3 years. When leadership changes, Six Sigma vanishes. Meanwhile every company and consultant is still using the time-honored but flawed top-down, all-or-nothing strategy for implementation. Over 50 years of research into how companies and cultures adopt changes like Six Sigma suggests that "to accelerate adoption you will want to REDUCE the number of people involved." Fewer people, faster implementation!

3. Six Sigma is under performing the media hype

- 64% of respondents agreed that Six Sigma had significantly improved profitability.
- 50% agreed that Six Sigma had improved customer satisfaction.
- Only 43% agreed that Six Sigma had improved job satisfaction among employees.

OUCH! This means that current approaches to implementing Six Sigma are delivering a paltry 2-sigma performance (30% failure). No wonder we're looking at so many companies abandoning Six Sigma. The companies that are getting results are doing something different. What is it?

4. You don't need Black Belts to get results
80% agreed that you should use whatever tools are necessary to get the job done. But, when asked which methods and tools yielded the greatest results, survey respondents answered:

- 87% cause-effect analysis (line, pareto, fishbone)
- 35% process mapping (flowcharts)
- 26% Lean manufacturing (value-added analysis)
- 20% Statistical process control (flowcharts, control charts, and histograms).

Stop Working *In* Your Business, Start Working *On* Your Business

I recently went into Sears to order a dishwasher and a TV. I got the part numbers and went to one of checkouts in appliances. They said that they could order the dishwasher, but not the TV. I'd have to go to the TV department to order the TV. The TV department wanted to charge me twice to have it delivered on the same day as the dishwasher. Doesn't this sound stupid to you? Shouldn't I have been able to order both at the same time?

Have you ever walked into someone else's business and almost immediately noticed some way that they could improve their operation to be better, faster or cheaper? Why haven't they noticed what you find obvious?

The answer isn't obvious: they're busy working *in* their business, but they rarely ever step out and work *on* their business.

People vs Process

People-oriented companies focus their attention on *who* is doing the job. They think: "If I could only get the right person in this job, everything would be peachy." Great people come at a premium price and when they leave they take their process with them.

Process-oriented companies focus on developing and following the right process. They depend on good processes to produce superior results. With a great process, you can hire and train the lowest skill level people available. If the Air Force can teach 18-year-olds with a high school diploma to maintain $30 million jets, you can too.

Remove the Speed Bumps

We all get trapped mentally inside of our companies because we spend so much time working *in* them. It takes some mental gymnastics to learn how to step outside of the business, to get some distance from it, so that you can work *on* the business and its processes.

Six Sigma is the best toolkit for helping you think outside the business. The tools are designed to help employees see the business more clearly than ever before.

Don't Reinvent the Wheel

Years ago, when I first got started with Six Sigma (a.k.a. TQM), we used a top-down, CEO-driven, all-or-nothing approach to implementation, just like companies are doing with Six Sigma today. Following the guidance of our million-dollar consultants, we started and trained hundreds of teams that met for one hour a week. Two years later only a handful of teams had successfully solved a key business problem. Most were mired in the early steps of the problem solving process.

So I decided to try something radical: I applied TQM (now known as Six Sigma) to TQM. I looked at:

- Each stuck team as a "defect."
- The "delays" built into process: the delays between training and application and the delays between team meetings.

I researched and found better methods for doing everything involved in implementation.

1. Using just-in-time (JIT) training, I was able to close the gap between learning and application.

2. Using one-day root cause teams, I was able to eliminate the delay between team meetings. Solutions that used to take months, now took only hours.

3. Using the power of "diffusion", I was able to weave the methods and tools of Six Sigma into the organization with a minimum involvement of key resources.

4. Using root cause analysis, I was able to streamline and simplify the process of focusing the improvement so that we only started teams that *could* succeed. You see, Six Sigma, like TQM before it, is a data-driven process. **If you don't have data about the problem, Six Sigma just won't work.** You don't have to have perfect data; there's no such thing, but you do have to have data that can narrow your focus. If not, you're lost.

By systematically applying Six Sigma to Six Sigma, I found ways to eliminate the failures and accelerate the delivery of results. That's what I call Six Sigma Simplified.

What is Six Sigma?

The Acronyms Have Been Changed

Over the years, I've had a chance to learn and study just about every "brand name" systematic improvement methodology. Guess what...*they are all pretty much the same.* To appear different, consultants have changed:

• the name to Six Sigma (from TQM)
• the acronyms to confuse the unwary (PDCA to DMAIC)
• the number of tools required for success
• the number of steps in the process (5 to 14 steps), but...

• **the key tools are the same**
• **the process for using the tools is the same**
• **and the results are identical** assuming you can figure out how to use the wide range of tools and processes.

For these minor, cosmetic differences consultants often charge huge *licensing* fees and you spend weeks in training just to get started. Is it any wonder that only big companies with deep pockets attempt to use these archaic methods?

How is Six Sigma Different from TQM?

It's not. The underlying tools and processes are the same. Ideally, the focus should shift from

• teams and training to *profits and productivity*;
• incremental improvement to *breakthrough improvement with bottom-line benefits.*

How is Six Sigma Simplified Different?

1. You get the essential tools necessary to achieve the desired result, not a bunch of tools that are only used in rare cases.

2. You get the most streamlined, elegant process I have ever found for breakthrough improvement.

3. You get the fastest, just-in-time training method that I've found for developing skill *and* delivering results in a matter of days, not weeks or months.

4. You get an easy-to-use tool kit to automate all of your Six Sigma activities (the QI Macros for Excel).

5. You save a small fortune in training and licensing fees, because there are none.

What is Six Sigma?

If we applied Six Sigma to ...

- Tax returns, there would only by 340 defects in the 100 million returns filed each year.

- Teen pregnancy—there would only be 34 pregnancies a year instead of 1,000,000.

- There would only be 3.4 accidents for every 1,000,000 miles driven.

- There would only be 3.4 deaths per million hospital admissions instead of 1 per 100 as reported by the National Academy Press.

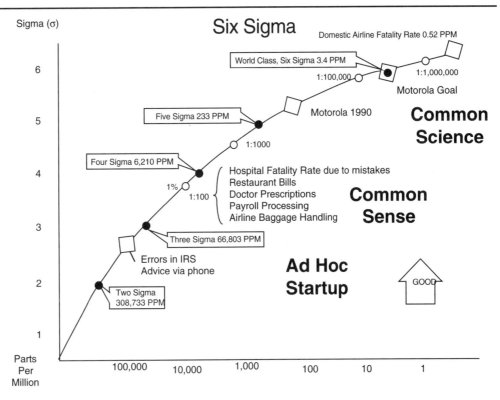

What Is Six Sigma?

What is Six Sigma? Six Sigma is a results-oriented, project-focused approach to quality. It's a way of measuring and setting targets for reductions in product or service defects that is directly connected to customer requirements. These reductions in the cost of poor quality translate into cost savings and competitive advantage. Sigma, σ, represents one standard deviation from the average or mean. Most control charts set their range at ±3σ, but Six Sigma extends three more standard deviations. At six sigma, there are only 3.4 parts per million (PPM) defective.

Why Six Sigma? Why now? For the last few years, GE and other large companies have been applying Six Sigma to improve performance. In 1998, GE invested $450 million to achieve $2 billion in savings (Wall Street Journal, April). In 2003, Six Sigma Qualtec reported helping their clients save over a billion dollars. Other Six Sigma pioneers are reporting significant savings. So, other Fortune 500 companies are following suit.

What is Six Sigma?

Fortune 500 corporations invested millions in TQM during the late '80s and early '90s, with little to show for it. Unfortunately, the intuition to learn improvement methods was right on, but the implementation was often wrong.

You don't have the time or money to inch your way to world-class; you have to make a number of "quantum leaps."

Six Sigma Targets

Sigma (σ)
Defects/Million

1	690,000
2	308,733
3	66,803
3.5	Average
4	6,210
5	233
6	3.4

Most business processes produce about 2-3% errors or 20-30,000 defects per million. Relying on incremental (10%) improvements to get you to world-class quality would take an infinite period of time. Four Sigma is 6,210 defects per million—an 80% reduction. Five Sigma is only 233 defects/million—an additional 96% reduction. Six Sigma is 3.4 defects per million—an additional decrease of 98%. Continuous improvement won't get you to Six Sigma, but Breakthrough Improvement will!

I'm not suggesting you throw away what you know or what you've learned so far; I'm suggesting an approach to implementation that you might want to consider if you want your investment in Six Sigma to payoff.

What is DMAIC?

As soon as someone mentions Six Sigma, they'll most likely regurgitate a series of acronyms that baffle everyone. The most frequently used acronym is DMAIC.

DMAIC is the latest in a long line of acronyms to describe the improvement process.

Define

The first step of the DMAIC process is to **define** the problem to be solved and the objectives for improvement. This involves understanding the customer's needs and how to **measure** these "critical to quality" (CTQ) requirements. This is also the place to analyze the "cost of poor quality."

Measure

The second step is to **measure** the current state of the process using the CTQs. Is it stable and capable (i.e., predictable) or unpredictable? This step invariably uses line or control charts.

Analyze

The third step is to **analyze** and verify the root causes of the problem. For most non-manufacturing applications, this involves little more than a pareto chart and a fishbone diagram. In manufacturing applications this may involve design of experiments (DOE), failure modes and effects analysis (FMEA), measurement systems analysis (MSA) and hypothesis testing.

Improve

The fourth step is to implement the **improvements** and confirm the results. This step uses flowcharts, control charts and histograms.

Control

The fifth step is to monitor and **control** the process using control charts and histograms.

PDCA vs DMAIC

Customers often ask me, what's the relationship between Shewhart's PDCA model and DMAIC. Because I started using a more simple acronym, FISH, long before Six Sigma even existed, here's my take on the map between all three:

PDCA	DMAIC	FISH
Plan	Define & Measure	Focus
Do	Analyze	Improve
Check	Improve	
Act	Control	Sustain
		Honor

What is DFSS?
Building Quality Into Your Systems

Purpose

To design processes, products, and services to deliver Six Sigma quality *before* they are used.

Once you reach five sigma (233 defects/million), you may begin to reach the limits of what you can do with basic problem solving. At this point, you might consider redesigning your products, services, and processes to deliver Six Sigma quality right from the start. You can begin by *benchmarking* best practices from other companies or reengineering existing processes.

- **Benchmarking** involves studying the best practices of companies in other industries that already do certain things well. The internet, for example, routes packets of information. So does Federal Express. What do they have in common? If you need to route packets of information more effectively and efficiently, what could you learn from these two sources?

- **Reengineering** involves starting with the customer's requirements and redesigning your products, services, and the processes that create them to mistake-proof the entire system. This involves using Quality Function Deployment (QFD) and sometimes Design of Experiments (DOE).

Design for Six Sigma

FISH	Step	Activity
Focus	1	Identify process, product, or service to redesign
Improve	2	Benchmark best practices of other companies
	3	Use QFD to redesign core products, services, and processes
	4	Use DOE to optimize production parameters
Sustain	5	Prototype and problem solve to achieve optimal results
Honor	6	Recognize and reward team members.

Making Six Sigma Payoff

Right Idea, Wrong Leaders

In the 1990s, I was working in the phone company when our CEO "committed" to quality. Hundreds of millions of dollars and almost five years later, the company abandoned TQM. Having the CEO on your side may help, but it's not the holy grail of gaining organization-wide commitment to Six Sigma.

If you've read anything about Six Sigma, you've heard it repeated endlessly that you want to get top leadership commitment to Six Sigma. The emerging science of complexity suggests that this is a mistake. Getting CEO commitment invokes what complexity scientists call the Stalinist Paradox, which lowers your chances of success to 50:50.

The emerging science of networks suggests that it's *never* the formal leadership that determines the success or failure of a culture change...it's the *informal* leaders—the hubs—in any "network" that determine success. Informal networks are more like spiderwebs or wagonwheels, not hierarchies.

Formal Network

Informal Network

The Tipping Point

In *The Tipping Point*, Malcolm Gladwell argues that any idea "tips" into the mainstream when sponsored by one of three informal leaders: connectors, mavens, and salespeople.

Connectors connect people with other people they know. Think about your own company. Who is the center of influence that knows everybody and introduces everyone to everyone else?

Mavens connect people with new ideas. Who is the center of influence in your company who gets everyone on board with all the new changes in technology (e.g., Six Sigma, SPC, etc.).

Connectors and Mavens are what Seth Godin, the author of *Ideavirus*, calls the *powerful sneezers*—someone who spreads an ideavirus, because it enhances their status.

Salespeople are what Seth would call a "promiscuous sneezer." They do it for money. When you follow the CEO-commitment rule, these folks will show up like vultures to a carcass. Beware.

> To accelerate Six Sigma, leverage your informal leaders.

Making Six Sigma Payoff

Don't Confuse the Means with the Ends

Too many companies are losing sight of the objective when it comes to Six Sigma. The goal is to cut costs, boost profits, and accelerate productivity; it is not the wholesale implementation of the Six Sigma methodology.

At the American Society for Quality's annual conference, many people stopped by our booth drawn by the promise of Six Sigma *Simplified*. They'd been buried in an avalanche of conventional folklore that you have to make a major commitment to Six Sigma, spend lots of money training black belts, and wait years for results. Every one of these disheartened small business owners voiced the same questions: "Isn't there a better way?"

Of course there is, because all of the conventional wisdom and hype about Six Sigma is DEAD WRONG!

To increase results, narrow your focus.

The Goal is Bottom Line, Profit-Enhancing, Productivity Boosting Results!

Six Sigma is merely a means to that end. Nothing more. It is not the one-size-fits-all, universal cure to what ails your business. Six Sigma is a power toolkit for solving two key business problems:

- **defects**—errors, mistakes, scratches, imperfections
- **delay**—when the customer's order is idle

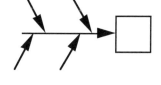

Six Sigma works very well on problems with *linear* cause-effects. If you step on the gas pedal in your car, for example, the car accelerates. This is a linear cause-effect.

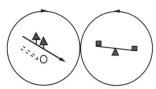

Six Sigma doesn't work well on problems with *circular or systemic* cause-effects. In other words, you can't use Six Sigma *directly* to change morale or customer satisfaction. If you engage employees in improving the business, morale may improve, or it may not. If you improve your products and services, customer satisfaction may improve, or it may not.

The Power Laws of Speed

In a global economy, everyone is competing against the clock. So, speed is critical to your success. In *Competing Against Time*, (Free Press 1990), the authors present compelling evidence for the power laws of speed:

The 5% Rule

The amount of time it takes to deliver a product or service is far greater than the actual time spent adding value to the product or service. Most products and services only receive value for 5% of the total delivery time. Why does it take so long? Delay. The product is sitting idle far too long between steps in the process.

Examples: A manufacturer of heavy vehicles only spends 16 hours assembling a vehicle, but 45 *days* preparing the order. A claims processing group only spends seven hours processing a claim, but it takes 140 days for each claim.

Remove the Speed Bumps

Idle time has three components:

1. Waiting to complete a "batch" of work as well as waiting on the batch ahead.
2. Rework of mistakes
3. Decision making

The 25-2-20 Rule

Every time you reduce the time required to provide a product or service by 25%, *you double productivity and cut costs by 20%.*

The 3X2 Rule

When you slash your cycle time to do mission-critical processes, you enjoy growth rates three times the industry average and twice the profit margins.

Value added flow analysis will help you find ways to eliminate the delays between each step of the process. Employees won't have to work any harder; you just eliminate the delay.

To increase results, narrow your focus.

The Power Laws of Quality

Even though every manager has heard the 80-20 rule, they still try to deploy Six Sigma everywhere. But Six Sigma is like peanut butter—the wider you spread it, the thinner it gets. Remember the dark side of the 80-20 rule: if you try to use Six Sigma everywhere, 80% of your effort will only produce 20% of the benefit.

Bell-Shaped Mindset

Because quality principles evolved predominantly in a manufacturing environment, there's a lot of emphasis on the "normal" or bell-shaped curve, where product measurements are distributed across a range of values. Unfortunately, this emphasis has blinded most leaders to the reality that defects tend to cluster in small parts of the process; they aren't spread all over like butter on bread.

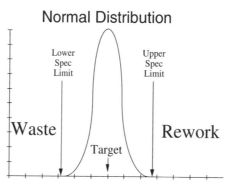

Normal Distribution

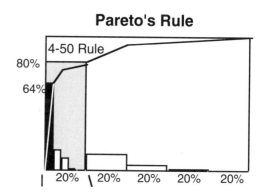

Pareto's Rule

To increase results, reduce the number of people involved.

What if you could get over half of the "benefit" from Six Sigma by investing in just 4% of the business? You can! Pareto's 80/20 rule is a power law. Power laws aren't linear, they grow by orders of magnitude. So, if you believe in Pareto's rule, you have to believe that it applies within the 20%: 4% of the business will cause 64% of the waste and rework. Wherever I go, I find that four percent of transactions cause over 50% of the rework. Four percent of Americans have over half the wealth.

Better still: The research into the diffusion of innovation shows that transformational change begins with less than five percent of the work force (4%). It also suggests that **to accelerate the implementation of Six Sigma you will want to reduce the number of people involved.**

Take The Low Road

Traditional Six Sigma wisdom says that you have to take an all-or-nothing, wall-to-wall approach to Six Sigma. This too is dead wrong. It's a myth spread by Six Sigma consultants (promiscuous sneezers) who directly benefit from it.

The Six Sigma world seems to be increasingly divided between the haves and the have nots, the Six Sigma snobs and the plebeian masses. The reigning wisdom seems to be that to succeed at Six Sigma, you have to embark on a total cultural transformation.

Sadly, I haven't heard anyone talking about the benefits they have achieved from implementing such a transformation, and the Quality Digest survey bears this out. There seems to be this illusion that if you embark on Six Sigma, you'll magically be transported to a place of productivity and profitability. Nothing can be further from the truth. I've heard too many stories of massive investment in Six Sigma with little return. One quality auditor expressed concern that if we aren't measuring the ROI of Six Sigma; we're just fooling ourselves. After you pony up an estimated $250,000 (training, salary, projects, etc.) to develop a Black Belt, are you going to get at least $50,000 a project?

So why are all of these big companies trying to do it the all-or-nothing way? Because you can't be criticized for aggressively doing everything possible to implement Six Sigma (even though the research says you should be punished for wasting so much money.)

To accelerate Six Sigma, reduce the number of people involved

There has to be a better way

There is a better way that produces better results with minimal risk: the crawl-walk-run strategy. First, use the research-based power of "diffusion" to implement Six Sigma: *start small* with the first 4% of your business that produces over 50% of the waste and rework (I'll explain how to do this later in the book), then the next 4%, and so on until you reach a critical mass. Then Six Sigma will sweep through the company, pulled forward by word of mouth. When I explain this "crawl-walk-run" approach to business owners, each one seems to awaken from his or her fog of despair and envision a path to Six Sigma that is doable.

Set BHAGs

In *Built To Last*, (Collins 1997), the authors mention the need for a BHAG or Big Hairy Audacious Goal. Using Six Sigma as a guide, you can measure your current performance in defects per million and set a BHAG of reaching the next level sigma.

So, if your computer system has 2% downtime, that's 20,000 minutes per million or about 3.5 sigma. Set a goal to reach 5 sigma (1 minute/5,000 minutes available)

Conventional wisdom suggests that the goal is incremental improvement. But if 4% of the business can produce over half the lost productivity and lost profit, why aren't you shooting for what Jim Collins, (*Built to Last* and *Good to Great*) calls a Big Hairy Audacious Goal (BHAG).

Service Example: One computer operations VP set a goal of a 50% reduction in on-line system downtime for the year. Even though no one thought it possible, the group reduced downtime by 74% in just six months using Six Sigma Simplified.

IT Example: One information systems VP set a goal to cut order errors in half over the year. The IT group reduced order errors from 17% to 3% in just four months using Six Sigma Simplified, an 82% improvement.

Set a BHAG to reduce defects in one of your mission critical systems by 50% in six months:

- Order errors
- Product or service defects
- Billing errors
- Purchase order errors
- Payment errors

Set a BHAG to reduce cycle time in a customer critical process by 50% in the next six months. You'll be surprised how far such a goal will take you.

Or, using Six Sigma as a guide, set the next level Sigma as a target. If you're at 3-Sigma, go for 4-Sigma, and so on. Your target for world-class quality is at least 5-Sigma (233 defects per million). And you can get there in 18-24 months using Six Sigma Simplified. If GE can save $2 Billion in one year by focusing on Six Sigma, how much could you save?

Use SWAT Teams

Instead of letting teams choose their focus, consider 2-day leadership meetings to define and select key objectives.

SWAT Teams

Instead of teams that meet indefinitely, consider having 2-day root cause "meetings" that bring together the right internal experts to focus on solving a critical business problem that affects customers and therefore profitability. These meetings focus on analyzing and verifying the root causes of problems and then identifying solutions.

There are "instant" solutions that can be implemented immediately by the meeting participants, and there are "managed" solutions that need some leadership and project management to ensure proper implementation.

You Can't Learn to Swim Without Getting Wet

Conventional wisdom suggests that you need to train at least one blackbelt. This means that you have to send one of your top people away for four weeks at a cost of $15,000 or more to get trained in all of the "just-in-case" tools and techniques of Six Sigma. This, of course, is another myth propagated by Six Sigma consultants who want you to spend money on training.

Sadly, many employees want the blackbelt training, not so that they can help the company, but so that they can fatten their resume and get a better job somewhere else. Bye bye investment!

I just got a request for proposal from a hospital to train their leaders and staff members. They wanted at least 20 staffers recognized as green belts and 20 recognized as black belts.

Big contract, lots of training. Sounds seductive, doesn't it?

Well, all that training is great for the trainer's pocketbook, but bad for customers. You end up with highly trained, accredited, but inexperienced improvement leaders. This lack of experience can kill Six Sigma. I suggested that what they really want are experienced professionals that can diagnose, treat, and heal issues concerning speed, quality of care, and costs.

The sad truth is that **you lose 90% of what you learn in a classroom if you don't use it within 48-72 hours**. And isn't that what happens: you go to training and come back after a week to a pile of work. By the time you're caught up, you can't remember what you learned just a few days ago.

To increase learning, decrease training

Looking at this from a Six Sigma perspective, the delay between training and application isn't just about the waste of time, but also about loss of skill. The only way to reengineer this problem is to eliminate the delay: **just-in-time training.**

In the early 1990s, when I was lured into the in-depth training paradigm, I'd spend a week using a Deming Prize Winning methodology to train 20 team leaders. They, in turn, would start teams that met once a week for an hour. Months went by. Years went by. Nothing got better.

You Can't Learn to Swim Without Getting Wet

2 Hour JIT Training

So, unbeknownst to my company leadership, I changed the process. I shortened the training down to a couple of hours. I would only teach it immediately prior to solving a real problem. Then, in a day or two, I'd guide the team to a solution. They got experience and the good feelings associated with success. Surprisingly, many of these team members could then apply the same tools and process to other problems with equal success. I discovered that I was creating highly skilled, but essentially untrained team leaders in a matter of one day. To strengthen their abilities, I'd occasionally conduct a one-day intensive to review what they'd learned through experience. This helped reinforce what they knew and fill in any gaps.

With one day of experience and a day of review training, I was accomplishing what the old-style week of training and endless meetings could not. And, we were getting bottom-line benefits simultaneously.

Sadly enough, by the time I figured this out, the Quality Department was on its last legs because it had failed to do more than waste time and money defining and measuring cumbersome, error-prone processes that needed major repair. A year later, the department was disbanded and the people laid off.

Don't let this happen to you. Consider using just-in-time training to prep your teams for immediate immersion in problem solving or SPC. Use real data. Use real problems. From the time we are born, we learn by watching other people do things. When you guide a team through the process, they learn an enormous amount just by watching you. Then reinforce what they've learned unconsciously with one-day review training.

You'll save your company time and money, get immediate results, encourage the adoption of Six Sigma by satisfied employees, generate good buzz, and have more fun.

Lesson plans for just-in-time training are included in the Six Sigma Simplified Instructor Guide (qimacros.com/instructor.html).

Make your training stick!

Ensuring Successful Implementation

Change Agent Role

What is your role in getting people to adopt Six Sigma? How can you make it more contagious?

1. Prevent too much "adoption" (i.e., adoption by people who could reject it or sabotage implementation) which, paradoxically, will speed up diffusion.
2. Develop the need for change
3. Exchange information
4. Diagnose problems
5. Create an intent in the employees to change
6. Translate that intent into action
7. Stabilize adoption and prevent discontinuance
8. Achieve self-renewing behavior.

"The greatest response to change agent effort occurs when opinion leaders adopt, which usually occurs somewhere between 3 and 16 percent adoption in most systems."

For a technology as powerful as Six Sigma, it sure seems to be taking a long time to develop acceptance in the global village. The average period for the universal adoption of an innovation is 25 years. Question is: "Is there a way to speed it up? Is there a way to make Six Sigma more contagious in your company?" I believe the answer is "Yes!" So I'd like to offer for your consideration some information about how contagious ideas spread, what we can learn from it, and how to apply it to Six Sigma.

For over 50 years, researchers have studied (i.e., modeled) how changes are adopted, adapted or rejected by societies and cultures. This research is readily available in The Diffusion of Innovations, by Everett Rogers (Free Press, 1995). Diffusion is a model for understanding social change. There are several characteristics of "innovations" like Six Sigma that can be adjusted to increase the speed of adoption–advantages, compatibility, complexity, trialability, and observability. You might think of these characteristics as a way to develop rapport with any group of people that represent a culture–corporations, departments, etc. There is a clear decision strategy people follow to decide to adopt, adapt, or reject an innovation. And there are various communication channels through which an innovation "infection" can spread, although the winner is one-to-one positive word of mouth. And the change agent (Six Sigma professional) plays a key role in the speed of adoption.

I would like to suggest that TQM failed to take root in some companies because the implementation failed to apply the lessons learned about diffusion–how changes are adopted by society. Let's use this change model as a filter for our experience. Along the way I'll suggest some possible ways to adjust our approach to increase the spread of Six Sigma.

Characteristics of Innovations

The Relative Advantage of Six Sigma

The heart of Six Sigma is about doing business better, faster, and cheaper. By letting customers get what they want, when they want it, at a price they perceive as offering superior value,

Accelerating Six Sigma

Adopter Categories

Innovators

(Explorers)–active seekers and champions of new ideas. They are intuitive and often perceived as deviant from the social system.

Early Adopters

(Colonists)–quickly notice shifts and begin to implement and improve them. Evangelists are essential for early adoption.

Early Majority

(Deliberate Settlers)– rely on the early adopters and opinion leaders to decide to adopt. These people need a coach.

Late Majority

(Skeptical Settlers)– These people won't adopt until it's safe. Neighbors from the early majority are important for later adopters.

Laggards

(Traditional) the corporate "immune system" will try to prevent a new idea from spreading.

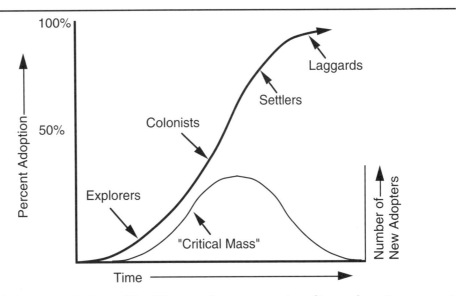

businesses thrive. Six Sigma, however, is often about preventing problems. Innovations involving prevention are slower to spread than innovations that solve pressing problems.

Compatibility - To be successful, any innovation must seek compatibility with a culture's:

• values and beliefs
• previously introduced ideas
• "felt" needs

Perhaps the most pervasive beliefs are that "we're working as hard as we can," as if working hard will solve the problem. This is a conscious "real world set of beliefs" that limit the adoption of Six Sigma.

Complexity - the degree to which an innovation is perceived as difficult to understand and use.

Because most people don't have a set of Six Sigma filters, they perceive the required math and graphics as complex and impenetrable. Six Sigma, for many people, invokes their limiting beliefs about their ability to learn, do math, or understand graphs. Howard Gardner's work on the seven intelligences suggests that only some of us are visual or mathematically oriented. To succeed, we must simplify and streamline Six Sigma and create a path for people to follow at their own rate of speed.

Six Sigma Simplified

Accelerating Six Sigma

Speed of Adoption

The **speed of adoption** can be affected by how it is done and who has the authority to make it happen. The adoption decisions (in order of speed of adoption):

Fastest: Optional–choices made by each individual (e.g., participation in Six Sigma)

Medium: Authority–made by one or a few people with power, status, or technical expertise.

Slowest: Collective–made by consensus of members

Varies: Combination of the above.

Trialability - new ideas, tried on the installment plan are easier to adopt because you can learn by doing.

People like to try things and then decide. Most employees want to make things better to serve customers more effectively. What else can we do to increase Six Sigma's trialability?

Observability - the ability to see results and for others to see them too.

This is a tough one, because the results of Six Sigma are often "invisible," because it prevents problems. There is often a delay between achieving better quality and increasing market share and profits. Recommendation: Find a way to make the effects of improvements "visible" to casual observers.

So those are the characteristics that can make Six Sigma more contagious–advantages, compatibility, complexity, trialability, and observability. Now let's look at the decision process used to adopt, adapt, or reject an innovation and the various types of adopters.

The Innovation-Decision Process

There is a step-by-step process people follow to decide to adopt, adapt, or reject a change or innovation in their lives:

1. First comes **knowledge** - an awareness/understanding of the problem. For me, this happened when the company decided to implement Six Sigma. This initial awareness involves:

• What is Six Sigma?
• How-to apply Six Sigma
• Why Six Sigma? -Principles underlying how it works
• Where might it apply in your life?

2. Next comes **persuasion**. I persuaded myself to learn Six Sigma. Other people need to be persuaded. How can we become the role models to influence more people to embrace Six Sigma?

3. Then comes the **decision**. Each person seeks information to decide whether to adopt or reject, either passively or actively, the change.

Accelerating Six Sigma

Communication Channels

A communication channel is a means by which messages get from one person to another.

Interpersonal Channels

These are a slower but more effective means of persuading people to adopt a new idea. Used in the persuasion stage, it can:

1. Provide two-way exchange of information.
2. Allow an individual to form or change strongly held attitudes or beliefs

Mass Media–TV, radio, and print–can:

1. Reach large audiences
2. Create and spread information quickly
3. Change weakly held attitudes

4. Then, assuming the person decided to adopt the change, they begin **implementation**. This sometimes requires adaptation of the change (e.g., applying Six Sigma in context of interest).

5. Finally, after a period of time, people achieve **confirmation**. They confirm for themselves that the change is a good one and that it deserves to stay. Or, they may reject it.

This decision process becomes increasingly complex when working with a system or group rather than one individual.

Consequences of Adopting Six Sigma

• **Desirable vs undesirable**–Six Sigma can help serve customers more effectively and grow market share, but it can also cause employee concerns. Six Sigma can also cost too much and deliver too little if we try to train everyone and implement too many teams.

• **Direct vs indirect**–the direct consequences of Six Sigma could be customer satisfaction (outcome) while indirect might be greater income (effect) from better personal and professional relationships.

• **Anticipated vs Unanticipated**–Will the gap between successful and unsuccessful companies grow as the successful use Six Sigma to develop greater marketshare? Will a focus on Six Sigma discourage innovation and product development?

Recommendation: Amplify the benefits and prepare for potential problems. If we don't anticipate, understand, and reframe people's concerns about the undesirable, indirect, and unanticipated consequences of adopting Six Sigma, we really aren't concerned with the success of the change, are we?

Conclusions

We've covered over 50 years of research on how to accelerate the adoption and application of Six Sigma through:

1. better presentation of the attributes of Six Sigma
2. understanding decisions and their effect on adoption
3. the power of mass media and personal communications

Six Sigma Simplified

The Improvement Journey

The tide of evolution carries everything before it.
   George Santayana

In the long run, the only sustainable source of competitive advantage is your organization's ability to learn faster than its competition.
   Peter Senge

All improvement efforts follow a simple, basic process: FISH–Focus, Improve, Sustain, and Honor. FISH recognizes that there is a cycle of breakthrough improvement. Six Sigma offers a systematic way to continuously improve every aspect of your business. Six Sigma begins with **focusing** effort for maximum benefit, then **improving** the processes, **sustaining** the improvement and **honoring** your progress.

Breakthrough Improvement

FISH	Step	Activity	DMAIC
Focus	1	Focus the improvement	Define & Measure
Improve	2	Reduce defects & delay	Analyze & Improve
Sustain	3	Sustain the improvement	Control
Honor	4	Recognize and refocus	

FOCUS Laser Focus

Most organizations suffer from diffused focus and conflicting objectives at all levels in the organization. To succeed with Six Sigma, organizations must shift from trying to do everything, to focusing on a few key issues that will move them the farthest toward satisfying customers.

Increase the Good

Decrease the Bad

All progress is based on the desire to move from a current level of success to a more desirable one–better quality, delivered faster and cheaper with a higher profit. Whether in business or your personal life, you will want to increase the good (profits and marketshare) and decrease the bad (waste or rework). To do both requires the application of resources. To move from the

Six Sigma Simplified
Focusing and Improving

current state of affairs to a higher, better state requires that a leader set the direction, and allocate the people, time, and money to make improvements happen.

Unfortunately, even in the smallest organizations, everyone has a different perception of what the desired state should be. To overcome this lack of focus, a leader needs to define the desired state–a vision of the desired outcomes and their effects using the balanced scorecard.

The world owes all its onward impulses to men ill at ease. The happy man inevitably confines himself within ancient limits.
  Nathaniel Hawthorne

Then, leadership can define the few key improvement objectives, measurements, and targets that serve as a compass for moving from the present state to the desired state. By linking these objectives throughout the company, identifying improvement projects, and deploying the right resources we can begin the journey toward the company's vision. Leadership will also identify the core business processes and initiate improvement projects to define and dramatically improve each process.

IMPROVE Double Your Quality!

The problem-solving process further focuses improvements on the <u>root causes</u> of any quality problem–defects, high cost, or long cycle times. Preventing a root cause eliminates the symptoms, which ensures better products or services, increased customer satisfaction, and higher profits.

A process that <u>can meet</u> the customer's needs at least some of the time will benefit from using the problem-solving process. A small reduction of root causes will significantly reduce symptoms and dramatically increase the positive effects of the improvement.

IMPROVE Double Your Speed!

(a.k.a. Lean)

Improvement teams can then identify the process steps that add value and those that don't. In most processes, only one out of every four steps add value. The rest either delay the product or service, or deal with the waste and rework found along the way. Focusing on the steps that add value and eliminating the steps that don't, often yields dramatic improvements.

Six Sigma Simplified
Improving and Sustaining

IMPROVE Design for Six Sigma	A process that is not even remotely capable of meeting the customer's expectations will need to be replaced. Any process over five years old may benefit from benchmarking (borrowing best practices) or reengineering to simplify and automate.
Plans get you into things but you got to work your way out. Will Rogers	Benchmarking compares your current performance with internal groups or external companies that are the best in class at any particular activity. Benchmarking seeks to understand the difference and adapt it to meet your internal business needs. It requires that you understand your own processes and performance first; so SPC is a prerequisite.
Quality Function Deployment	QFD is a powerful tool for reengineering business processes or designing new products and services. QFD identifies key customer needs and the essential people, process, and technology necessary to fulfill those requirements.

SUSTAIN SPC

Improvement projects often begin by defining how work gets done–the present method of operation. SPC uses flowcharts and graphs to define the current process. Using the graphs, we can determine how "stable" or predictable the process is and how "capable" it is of meeting our customer's requirements.

Defined   **Stable**   **Capable**

HONOR

Throughout the improvement process, take time to celebrate, recognize, and reward improvement in both results and the application of Six Sigma.

Laser Focus

The Power of Focus

Pareto's Rule

Each element of Six Sigma focuses on the key leverage points in the business–the "vital few." This is the essence of Pareto's rule: 20% of what you do yields 80% of the results.

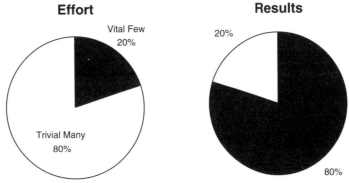

Process	Defects Time Cost
20 %	80%
4%	64%
1%	50%

Pareto's Rule states that 20% of your effort delivers 80% of the results. Six Sigma seeks to identify the "vital few" areas that will deliver the most return on investment. 20% of your customers, for example, generate 80% of your revenue.

The 4-50 Rule

Pareto's rule can be applied to itself. 4% of your effort (20% of the 20% of the vital few) will yield 64% of the results (80% of the 80%). Using data, Six Sigma narrows your focus to create the maximum benefit for the minimum effort.

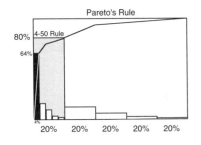

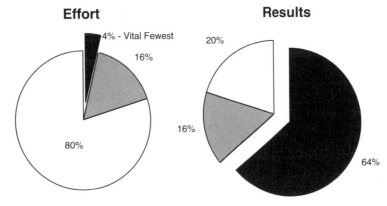

Breakthrough Improvement

- 50% of TQM fails
- Reason: Focus
- 4-50 rule: 4% of process creates over 50% of the waste and rework.

Even further, 1% of your effort will yield 50% of the result. For this reason, 50% improvements (a goal set with good old Yankee spirit) are often possible.

As you can see, you don't have to be perfect and fix everything, you just have to be able to focus on the vital few.

Laser Focus
(Define and Measure)

Focus

All improvements involve moving from a present way of satisfying customers to a more desired method. Before we can set the improvement processes in motion, however, we first have to define our direction for improvement. Where most improvement teams fail is in getting properly focused. To succeed, you will want to focus on your customer's needs and follow the data.

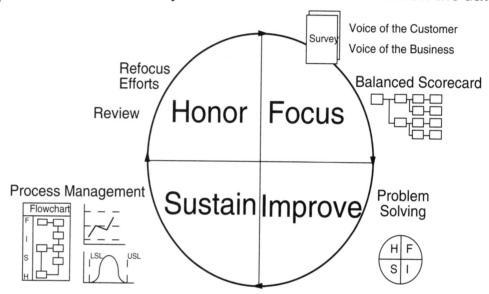

Process

Focus	Step	Activity
Define	1	Use the Voice of the Customer, business, and employee to identify desired long- and short-term objectives, and develop a balanced scorecard.
Measure	2	Identify and track the indicators
	3	Set targets (BHAGs) for improvement

Identify Requirements
Voice of The Customer

**Gather
The Voice**

*The reason why we
have two ears and
only one mouth is that
we may listen the
more and talk the less.*
Zeno of Citium
(c. 300 B.C.)

Purpose: to gather the customer's needs and
wants as a basis for establishing objectives.

Only customers can create jobs. So customer satisfaction is a
central theme of Six Sigma. There are *direct* customers (e.g.,
actual buyers or retailers) and *indirect* customers (e.g., govern-
ment regulatory agencies). Each customer has unique requirements which can be related to the business.

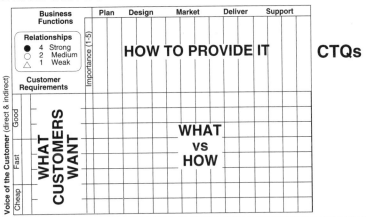

Process

Step	Activity
1	Identify your direct and indirect customers
2	Get the direct customer's requirements from surveys, focus groups, interviews, complaints, and correspondence. Review indirect customer requirements(e.g., regulations, laws, codes, etc.) Use the affinity diagram to combine the direct and indirect customer requirements into critical to quality (CTQ) elements
3	Enter key customer voice statements on left. Have customers rate the importance from 1 (low) to 5 (high).
4	Identify and enter key business functions for delivering the customers requirements along the top.
5	For each box in the center, rate the contribution of the "how" (top) to the "what" (left). Multiply the importance times the relationship weight to get the total weight. ● = Strong ○ = Medium △ = Low
6.	Total the columns. The highest scores show where to focus your improvement efforts.

Identify Requirements
Voice of the Customer

VOC

The Voice of the Customer uses *their* language to describe what they want from your business. Using a restaurant as an example to elicit the participant's "voice of the customer" for dining experiences, ask:

When you go into a restaurant, what do you want?

Good	Get my order right
	I want good food
	I want an accurate bill
	Give me payment options—cash, check, credit card
Fast	Greet me and seat me promptly
	Serve me promptly
	Serve my food <u>when I want it</u> (fast or slow)
	Have my check ready
Cheap	Give me good value for money spent
	Don't waste food

How do restaurants provide the meals? Greet & seat, take orders, prepare & serve food, bill, collect. What are the most important processes?

Restaurant

Relationships
- ● 4 Strong
- ○ 2 Medium
- △ 1 Weak

Voice of the Customer (direct & indirect)

Customer Requirements			Importance (1-5)	Greet	Seat	Take Drink Order	Take Food Order	Order Supplies	Prepare Order	Serve Order	Customer Check	Take Payment
Good	Get my order right		5			●	●		●	○		
	I want good food		5						●	○		
	I want an accurate bill		4			●	●				●	
	Give me payment options		3									●
Fast	Greet me and seat me promptly		4	●	●							
	Serve me promptly		5			●	●					
	Serve my food when I want it		5						●	○		
	Have my check ready		4								●	
Cheap	Give me good value for money spent		4					○	●	○		
	Don't waste food		3						●			
				4	4	12	12	6	16	8	8	4

(Column groups: **Greet**, **Order**, **Prepare**, **Serve**, **Bill & Collect**)

Identify Requirements
Voice of the Customer

VOC Table   Using the form below, explore the interactions between the customer's requirements and your business.

Relationships
- ● 4 Strong
- ○ 2 Medium
- △ 1 Weak

Business Functions

Customer Requirements

Importance (1-5)

Voice of the Customer (direct & indirect)

Customer Requirements	Importance (1-5)	Plan		Develop		Market		Deliver		Support	
Good											
Treat me like you want my business											
Give me products that meet my needs											
Products/services that work all the time											
Be accurate, right the first time											
If it breaks, fix it right the first time											
Fast											
I want it **when** I want it											
Make commitments that meet my needs											
Meet your commitments											
I want fast easy access when I need help											
Don't waste my time											
If it breaks, fix it fast											
Cheap											
Charge prices that are fair, competitive											
Help me save money											
Total Weight											

QI Macros template: vocmtrx.xlt

   Six Sigma Simplified

Improvement Focus
Identify The Critical To Quality Indicators

Purpose

Define specific ways to measure the customer's requirements and to predict the stability and capability of the process.

CTQs

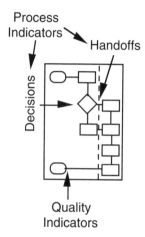

All problems invariably stem from failing to meet or exceed a customer's requirement. To begin to define the problem, you need to identify your customer's needs and a way to measure them *over time*–by hour, day, week, or month.

CTQs measure how well the product or service meets the customer's requirements. **Process indicators**, strategically positioned at critical hand off points in the process, provide an early warning system. For each CTQ there should be one or more process indicators that can predict whether you will deliver what your customers require.

Goodness is uneventful. It does not flash, it glows.
- David Grayson

A stone thrown at the right time is better than gold given at the wrong time.
Persian Proverb

Men go shopping just as men go out fishing or hunting, to see how large a fish may be caught with the smallest hook.
-Henry Ward Beecher

	Indicators		
Requirement	**CTQ or Process**		**Period**
Better	Number of defects Percent defective (number of defects/total)		minute hour day
Faster	# or % of commitments missed time in minutes, hours, days		week month
Cheaper	cost per unit cost of waste or rework		shift batch

There are usually only a few key customer requirements for any product or service. Identify your main supplier, customer, the product or service used, and the process that creates it. Begin by identifying your requirements of the supplier. Then, identify your customer's requirements for the product or service. What do they want in terms of good, fast, and cheap. Then, based on your customer's needs, identify how you can measure it with defects, time, or cost. Finally, identify how often you will measure: by minute, hour, day, week, or month.

 Six Sigma Simplified

Improvement Focus
Identify The Critical To Quality Indicators

Here are examples from three different environments to demonstrate how to identify the indicators based on requirements. For a restaurant, software developer, or telephone company who are your:

Main customers? diners, application users, people
Main products/services? food & drink, software, connection
Main Processes? ordering, preparation, delivery, billing

Type	Restaurant	Software	Telephone Company
GOOD	Right Food Right Temp Fresh Friendly	Easy-to-use Bug free Accurate	Good sound quality Worldwide access
FAST	Prompt • seating • service • check	When I want it Timely Updates Fix it fast	Be responsive Available when I want it If it breaks, fix it fast
CHEAP	Value for $ Stop Waste	Value for $	Value for $ Help me be effective

Six Sigma Simplified

Improvement Focus
Identify The Critical To Quality Indicators

Exercise

Purpose:
Measures

Agenda:

- Supplier
- Customer

Limit: 30 minutes

Hint: It's often easier, as a customer, to first identify what you want from a supplier, then to identify what your customers want.

For improvement efforts to be successful, they must focus on the customer's requirements and ways to measure them—defects, time, or cost.

Purpose: Develop your own CTQs

Agenda:

- Identify one key supplier and one key customer.

- First, for one supplier, identify one requirement for good, fast, and cheap. Identify how you would measure the supplier's quality.

- Next, select one requirement for good, fast, and cheap from the Voice of the Customer. Identify a CTQ for this requirement.

- Continue to expand your improvement story by adding the measures and any targets for improvement. If you're at three sigma, can you target four sigma? If you're at four, can you target five sigma?

Limit: 30 minutes

Improvement Focus
Identify The Critical To Quality Indicators

Main: **Supplier** _____

Customer _____

Product or Service _____

Process _____

Type	Requirement	Measurement	Period
Better		<u>Defects per million</u> (outages, inaccuracies, errors) <u>Defective per million</u> (scrap, rework, complaints) <u>Percent defective</u> (number defective/total)	
Faster		<u>Commitments missed</u> <u>Time to design, develop, deliver, repair or replace</u> <u>Wait or idle time</u>	
Cheaper		<u>Cost of rework or repair</u> <u>Cost of waste or scrap</u> <u>Cost per unit</u>	

Example

	Requirement	Measurement	Period
Better	What I want	Number of incorrect customer orders	Week
Faster	When I want it	Number of missed delivery commitments	Day
Value	Reduce my costs	Cost of correcting inaccurate orders	Day

QI Macros template: measures.xlt

Laser Focus
Create a Balanced Scorecard

Balanced Scorecard

A Balanced Scorecard links all of your efforts to ensure Breakthrough Improvements, not just incremental ones. The easiest way to depict this is with the "tree" diagram.

A balanced scorecard begins with a vision of the ideal world. This vision is then linked to long-term customer requirements, short term objectives, measures, and targets.

Key Tools

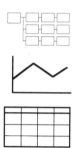

What's Important About A Balanced Scorecard?

1) If leadership does it, they will commit to achieving it.

2) It links customer needs to the improvement efforts. This clear linkage, which is often missing, helps employees and leaders focus on the customer and align all of their actions to achieve customer outcomes, not internally generated ones.

3) Measurements based on customer requirements provide an ideal way to evaluate performance.

4) Detailed balanced scorecards can then be developed and linked to this one by individual managers.

5) Results can be measured and monitored easily.

Long Term Objectives

Long Term Customer Requirements invariably fall into one of three categories (from the voice of the customer matrix):

- Better Quality–reliability and dependability
- Faster Service–speed and on time delivery
- Higher Perceived Value–lower cost

Short Term Objectives

Short Term Objectives translate these customer "fluffy" objectives into more concrete ones that can be **measured** and improved to meet the targets (from indicators):

- Better Quality–fewer defects in delivered products, services,
- Faster Service–reduced cycle time or missed commitments
- Higher Perceived Value–greater benefits achieved by reducing the cost of waste and rework.

Targets

Targets are the BHAGs (Big Hairy Audacious Goals as James Collins calls them in *Built To Last*) that challenge our creativity and ability. 50% reductions in cycle time, defects, and costs are both challenging and achievable in a one year period. But to do so requires highly focused, not random, improvement work.

 Six Sigma Simplified

Laser Focus
Create a Balanced Scorecard

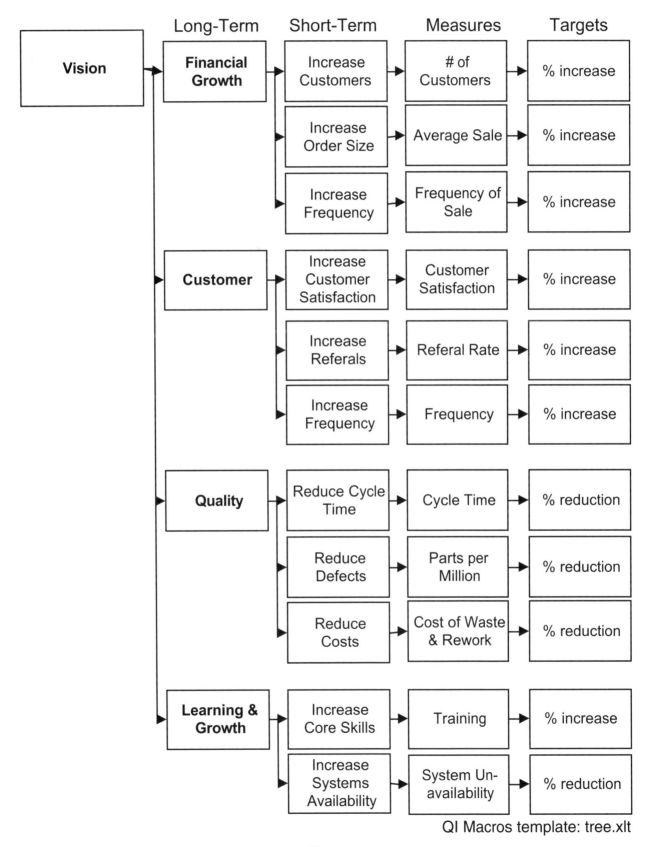

	Long-Term	Short-Term	Measures	Targets
Vision	**Financial Growth**	Increase Customers	# of Customers	% increase
		Increase Order Size	Average Sale	% increase
		Increase Frequency	Frequency of Sale	% increase
	Customer	Increase Customer Satisfaction	Customer Satisfaction	% increase
		Increase Referals	Referal Rate	% increase
		Increase Frequency	Frequency	% increase
	Quality	Reduce Cycle Time	Cycle Time	% reduction
		Reduce Defects	Parts per Million	% reduction
		Reduce Costs	Cost of Waste & Rework	% reduction
	Learning & Growth	Increase Core Skills	Training	% increase
		Increase Systems Availability	System Un-availability	% reduction

QI Macros template: tree.xlt

Double Your Speed!
(to reduce delay)

Lean Six Sigma

There is always a best way of doing anything.
              -Emerson

Why Go Lean?
5% Rule
Products receive value only 5% of the time.

25-2-20 Rule
Reduce cycle time by 25% to double productivity and cut costs by 20%.

3X2 Rule
Cut cycle time to enjoy growth rates three times industry average and twice the profit margins.

One of the best ways to improve your process is to find and eliminate as much of the delay as possible. Although the people are busy, the customer's order is idle up to 90% of the time—sitting in queue waiting for the next worker. Delay occurs in two main ways:

- Delays *between* steps in a process
- Delays caused by large batch sizes

So the obvious answer is to eliminate delays by:
1. Creating a continuous flow or "pull" system
2. Reducing batch size (to one if possible). Toyota, for example, can produce up to nine different cars on the same production line simultaneously customizing each one produced.

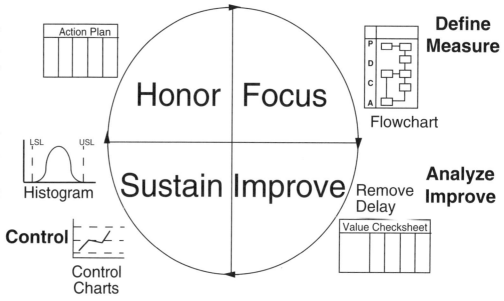

Process

FISH	Step	Activity
Focus	1	Define the process
	2	Identify the idle (i.e., wasted) time in the process (typically in the arrows)
Improve	3	Reduce or eliminate idle time

Double Your Speed!

The employees are busy, but ...

Big Batches → Activity 1 → Activity 2 → Activity 3

in — in — in — out

the order is idle 95% of the time

Reduce Delay!

Delay is caused by:

- Idle time between steps.

- Big batch sizes—work in progress (WIP)

- Rework to fix defects before, during, or after delivery.

- Time wasted creating products, services, or projects that end up being scrapped or cancelled.

This is what the process looks and feels like to your customer.

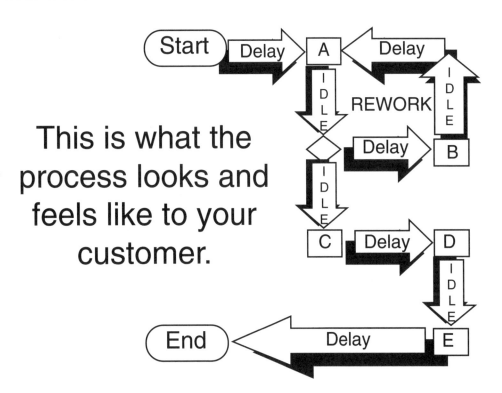

Six Sigma Simplified

Double Your Speed!
Define The Process Flow

Eliminate Waste and Rework

How long does it take to build a 3-bedroom, two bath, two car garage home with all of the plumbing, fixtures, paint, carpet, and landscaped yard?

There is an annual contest to build a house as fast as possible. **Last year's record was two hours and 48 minutes.** They do it by taking all of the idle time out of the process, combining steps, and getting all of the construction steps in the right order.

Value-added flow analysis assumes that <u>an idle resource is a wasted resource</u>. An activity or step that doesn't in some way directly benefit a customer is also wasteful. Rework, fixing stuff that's broke, is one of the more insidious forms of non-value added work: the customer wants you to fix it, but they really didn't want it to break in the first place.

Everyone is busy, but the order is idle:

• Requests for change may spend months in a prioritization cue before being worked (non-value added.)

• An order may sit idle waiting on an approval or material

On a process flow chart, **most of the non-value added time will be found in one of three places**:

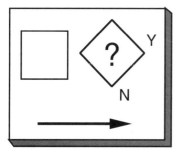

- **the arrows** (delay between process steps)
- **rework loops** (fixing errors that should have been prevented)
- **scrap processes** (discarding or recycling defective products)

To eliminate these non-value added activities, how can you:

- eliminate or reduce delay between steps?
- combine job steps to prevent wasteful delay?
- initiate root cause teams to remove the source of the rework?

Double Your Speed!
Define The Process Using A Flowchart

Purpose	Define the <u>existing</u> process as a starting point to begin improvement

Flowchart Symbols	A flowchart uses a few simple symbols to show the flow of a process. The symbols are:

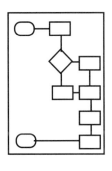

(rounded rectangle)	Start/End	Customer initiated
Do It (rectangle)	Activity	Adding value to the product or service (action verb & noun) (4% cause over 50% of defects)
? (diamond) Y / N	Decision	Choosing among two or more alternatives (beware of rework loops)
→ Arrow	Arrow	Showing the flow and transition (up to 90% of wasted/idle time)

The unified process of drawing and shooting was divided into sections: grasping the bow, nocking the arrow, raising the bow, drawing and remaining at the point of highest tension, loosing the shot.
  - Eugen Herrigel

Instead of writing directly on the flowchart, use square Post-it® notes for both the decisions and activities. This way, the process will remain easy to change until you have it clearly and totally defined. Limit the number of decisions and activities per page. Move detailed subprocesses onto additional pages.

Across the top of the flowchart list every person or department that helps deliver the product or service. Along the left-hand side, list the major steps in your process. In general, most processes have four main steps: planning, doing, checking, and acting to improve. Even going to the grocery store involves creating a list (plan), getting the groceries (do), checking the list, and acting to get any forgotten item. Virtually all effective business processes include these four steps.

Double Your Speed!
Define The Process

Process Flowcharts

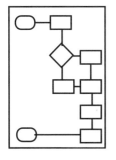

Process flowcharts extend the flowcharting technique to show "who does what" across the top of the flowchart and the macro steps of the process down the left-hand column. (See next page.) Guidelines for constructing process flow charts include:
- Start with identifying customer needs and end with satisfying them.
- Use the top row to separate the process into areas of responsibility.
- Use Post-it™ notes to lay out activities.
- Place activities under the appropriate area of responsibility.

Tips

Flowcharting

- Use square Post-it notes for activities and decision diamonds.
- Draw arrows on any size Post-it note to show the flow, top to bottom, left to right.
- Use smaller Post-it notes for process and quality indicators.
- Participants will often offer activities at different levels of detail. As the higher level process flow gets more complex, keep moving subprocesses onto micro process diagrams.

CTQs

- Quality indicators (CTQs) which measure how well the process met the customer's requirements go at the <u>end</u> of the process.

Process indicators

- Process indicators which predict how well the process will meet the requirements are most often placed at: 1) hand-offs between functional groups and 2) at decision points to measure the amount work flowing in each direction (this is most often useful for measuring the amount of rework required).

Double Your Speed!
Define The Process Using A Flowchart

Who Step	FLOWCHART			
	Customer			
Plan	(Request for product or service)			
Do				
Check				
Act	(Delivery of product or service)			QI Macros template: flowchrt.xlt

Double Your Speed!
Using Value-Added Analysis

Purpose	Identify the waste, rework, and delay that can be eliminated from the process.

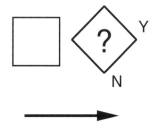

Over time, processes become cumbersome, inefficient, and ineffective. This complexity consumes more time and accomplishes less. Each activity, decision, and arrow on the flowchart represents time and effort. From the customer's point of view, little of this time and effort adds value; <u>most of it is non-value added</u>. From their point of view, delay and rework do not add value. We can increase productivity and quality by simplifying the overall process—eliminating delay and the need for rework.

Value Analysis

What we must decide is perhaps how we are valuable rather than how valuable we are.
-Edgar Z. Friedenberg

Everything is worth what its purchaser will pay for it.
- Publilius Syrus

What may be false in the science of facts may be true in the science of values.
- George Santayana

Step	Activity
1.	For each arrow, box, and diamond, list its function and the time spent (in minutes, hours, days) on the checklist.
2.	Now become the customer. Step into their shoes. As the customer, ask the following questions: • Is the order idle or delayed? • Is this inspection, testing, or checking necessary? • Does it change the product or service in a valuable way, or is this just "fix it" error correction work or waste?
3.	If the answer to any of these questions is "yes", then the step may be non-value added. If so, can we remove it from the process? Much of the "idle," non-value adding time in a process lies in the arrows: Orders sit in in-boxes or computers waiting to be processed, calls wait in queue for a representative to answer. How can we eliminate delay?
4.	How can activities and delay be eliminated, simplified, combined, or reorganized to provide a faster, higher quality flow through the process? Investigate hand-off points: how can you eliminate delays and prevent lost, changed, or misinterpreted information or work products at these points? If there are simple, elegant, or obvious ways to improve the process now, revise the flowchart to reflect those changes.

Double Your Speed!
Using Value-Added Analysis

			TIME SPENT (hours, days, weeks, months)	NON-VALUE ADDED? (Y/N)		
ACTIVITY, DECISION, or ARROW				IDLE TIME, WAIT TIME, OR DELAY?	INSPECT? DETECT? TEST?	REWORK? WASTE? SCRAP?

Value Checklist

QI Macros template: vafa.xlt

Example

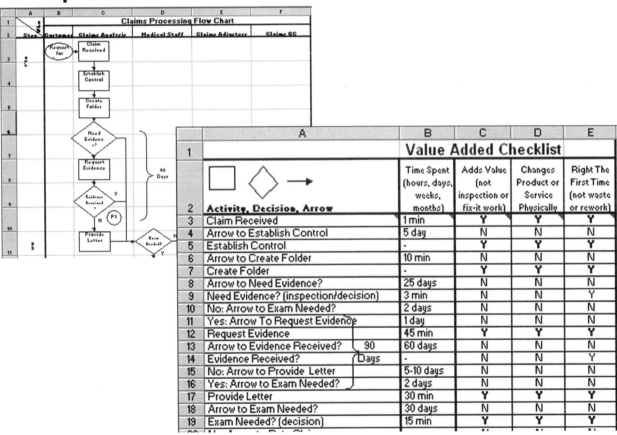

Double Your Quality!

Getting to Six Sigma	Most successful companies that have been around for more than five years are at about 3.5 sigma (1% defects). Most start-up companies, because of their ad hoc processes, are at 2.5 sigma (15-20% defects). I have found from experience that you don't need a lot of exotic Six Sigma tools to move rapidly up from these levels. You only need three basic tools: line, pareto, and fishbone. Companies I've worked with have used these tools to go from 2.5 to 3.5 sigma in about six months and 3.5 to 5 sigma in about two years. Once you get to 5 sigma, you'll be ready to use more exotic tools to design your work processes for Six Sigma. But until you get to 5 sigma, you may not have the discipline, desire, or rigor needed to use the more advanced tools.

Problem Solving

In this section, you'll learn how to apply the problem-solving process to achieve Six Sigma Improvements in speed, quality, and cost. The steps include:

- Define a problem for improvement using a line graph and pareto charts to select elements for improvement.
- Use the cause-and-effect diagram to identify root causes.
- Select countermeasures to prevent the root causes.
- Evaluate results from implementing the countermeasures.
- Find ways to replicate the improvement

Key Tools

There are <u>three key tools</u> in the problem-solving process:

- <u>Line graph</u> - to measure customer requirements
- <u>Pareto chart</u> - to <u>focus</u> the root cause analysis
- <u>Fishbone diagram</u> - to analyze the root causes of the problem or symptom

Double Your Quality!
Using the Problem Solving Process

Problem Solving

Our problems are man-made, therefore they may be solved by man. No problem of human destiny is beyond human beings.
  -John F. Kennedy

The **Six Sigma Problem Solving Process** also follows the FISH model–Focus, Improve, Sustain, and Honor. It focuses on identifying problems, determining their root causes, and implementing countermeasures that will reduce or eliminate the waste, rework, and delay caused by these problems.

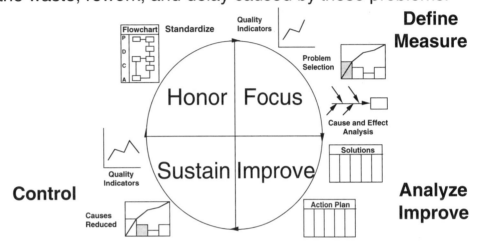

Process

The problem-solving process follows the FISH cycle to ensure breakthrough improvement:

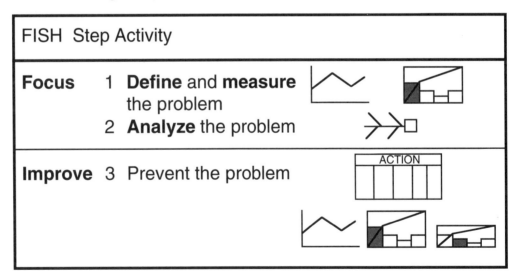

FISH	Step	Activity	
Focus	1	**Define** and **measure** the problem	
	2	**Analyze** the problem	
Improve	3	Prevent the problem	

Six Sigma Problem Solving
Step 1 - Define The Problem

Purpose	Define a specific problem area and set a target for improvement

Problems are only opportunities in work clothes.
  -Henry J. Kaiser

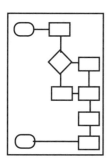

There are two ways of looking at problems:
  <u>Increase</u>   (want more of a "good" thing)
  <u>Decrease</u>   (want less of a "bad" thing)

These are often two sides of the same coin:

an increase in ...	is equal to a decrease in . . .
quality	number or percent defective
speed	cycle time–to deliver a product or service
	idle time–people, materials, machines
profitability	cost of waste and rework

Measurement

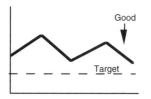

Solving problems is usually easiest when you focus on decreasing the "bad" rather than increasing the "good." Most problems can be easily expressed as a <u>line graph</u> showing the current trend and desired reduction in either cycle time, defects, or cost:

Example:

Pitfalls:
Starting a team with the wrong CTQ or poor focus.

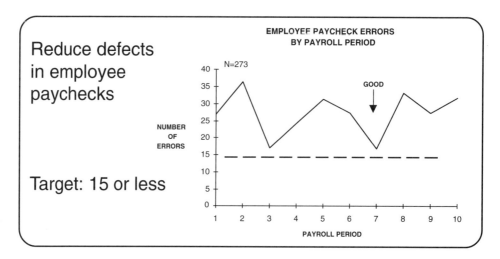

Reduce defects in employee paychecks

Target: 15 or less

Six Sigma Problem Solving
Step 1 - Define The Problem

(circle one)

Problem: Reduce   Defects   in

                Time   to deliver _____

                Cost   to deliver (product or service)

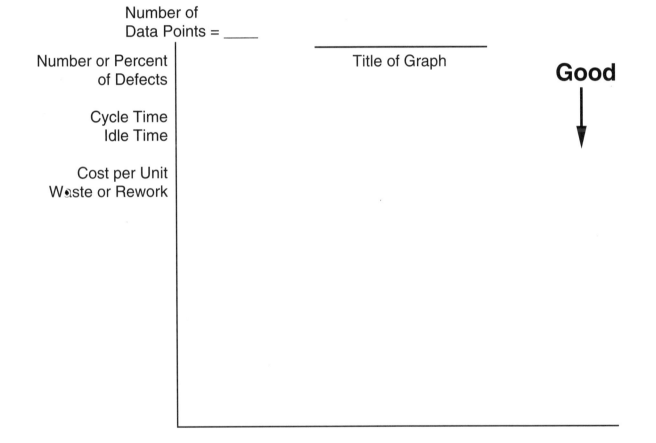

Number of
Data Points = ____

_____
Title of Graph

Number or Percent
of Defects

Cycle Time
Idle Time

Cost per Unit
Waste or Rework

Good

units (of time--hours, days, weeks) ⟶

| Who collected the data? |
| When was data collected? |
| Where? |
| What formula was used? |

QI Macros: Line or Run Charts

To automate all of your graphs, charts, and diagrams using Microsoft® Excel, get the *QI Macros For Excel.* *Download a Risk-FREE 30-day evaluation copy from* www.qimacros.com/freestuff.html

Six Sigma Improvement
Step 1 - Define The Problem

Pareto Chart

We only admit to minor faults to persuade ourselves that we have no major ones.
- La Rochefoucauld

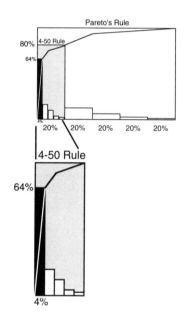

A problem well stated is a problem half solved.

Problem *areas* are usually too big and complex to be solved all at once, but when we whittle it down into small enough pieces, we can fix each one easily and effectively.

This step uses the Pareto chart (a bar chart and a *cumulative* line graph) to identify the most important problem to improve first.

Often, two or more pareto charts are needed to get to a problem specific enough to analyze easily. The left axis shows the number of occurrences for each bar. The right axis shows the cumulative percentage for the line graph.

Begin by identifying the components of the problem:

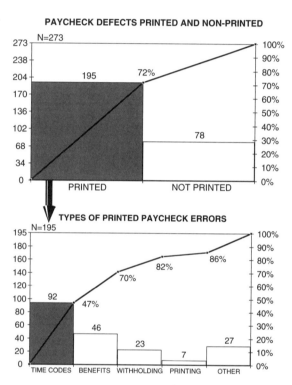

Indicator	Pareto Components
Defects	- types of defects
Time	- steps or delays in a process
Cost	- types of costs–rework, waste

Once we have whittled the problem down to a small enough piece, we can then write a problem statement about one or more big bars. This will serve as the basis for identifying root causes. We also need to set a target for improvement.

Problem Statement

Problem Statement: During the first five months of the year, time code errors accounted for 47% of all incorrect paychecks, which was 2X higher than the next highest contributor and resulted in 92 employee complaints.
Target: 50% reduction in time code errors

 Six Sigma Simplified

Six Sigma Improvement
Step 1 - Define The Problem

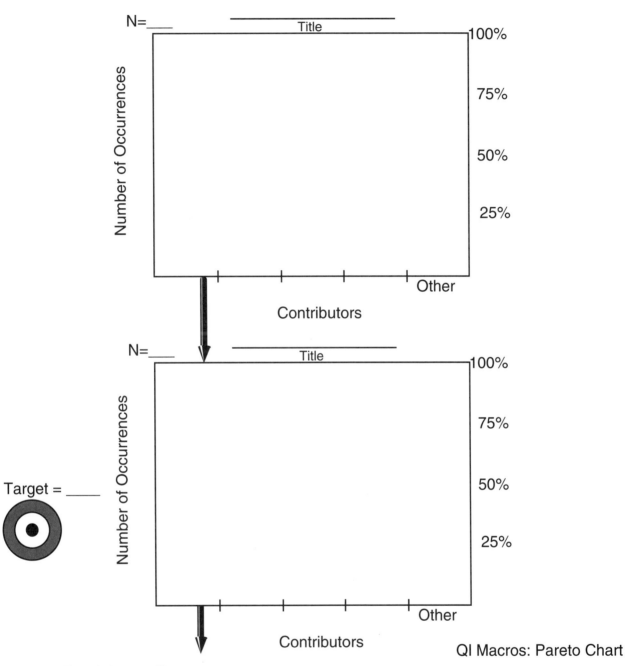

QI Macros: Pareto Chart

Problem Statement

During _____, _____, _____ accounted for ____% of _____,
      (Months)   (Year)   (Main Contributor)   (time, defects, cost)

which was ____ higher than desired and resulted in _____.
        (Gap)   (Pain)

Six Sigma Simplified

Six Sigma Improvement
Step 2 - Analyze The Problem

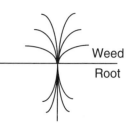

Weed
Root

Purpose

For every thousand hacking at the leaves of evil, there is one striking at the root.
-Thoreau

Identify and verify the root causes
   of the problem

Like weeds, all problems have various root causes. Remove the roots and, like magic, the weeds disappear.

Cause-Effect Analysis

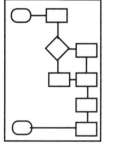

1. To identify root causes, use the fishbone or Ishikawa diagram. Put the problem statement from step 1 in the head of the fish and the major causes at the end of the major bones. Major causes include:

   • Processes, machines, materials, measurement, people, environment
   • Steps of a process (step1, step2, etc.)
   • Whatever makes sense

2. Begin with the most likely main cause.

3. For each cause, ask "Why?" up to five times.

4. Circle one-to-five <u>root</u> causes (end of "why" chain)

5. Verify the root causes with data (Pareto, Scatter)

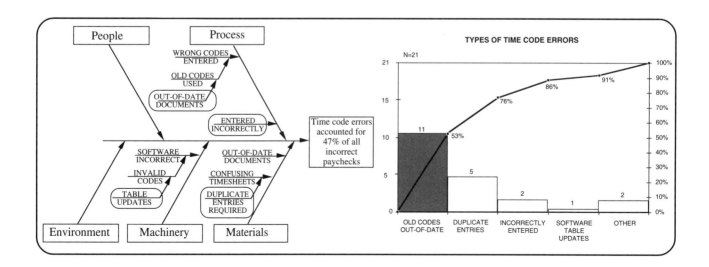

Six Sigma Improvement
Step 2 - Analyze The Problem

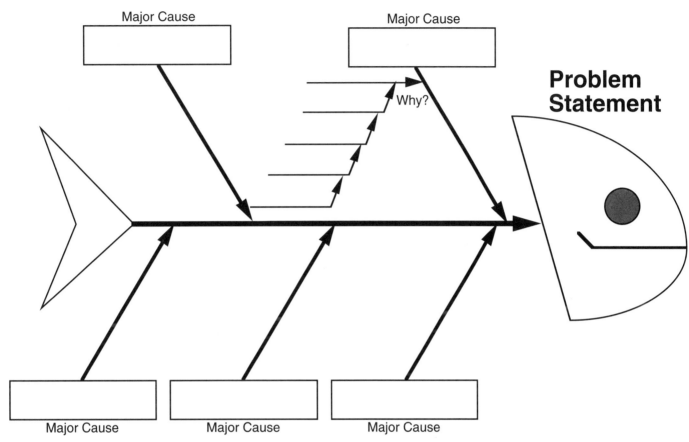

Major Cause

Major Cause

Problem Statement

Why?

Major Cause

Major Cause

Major Cause

QI Macros Template: Ishikawa diagram

Verification of Root Causes

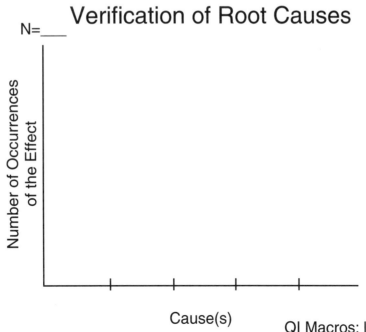

N=___

Number of Occurrences of the Effect

Cause(s)

QI Macros: line and pareto charts

Six Sigma Simplified

Six Sigma Improvement
Step 3 - Prevent The Problem

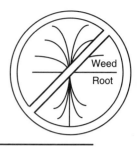

Purpose

Identify the countermeasures required to reduce or eliminate the root causes

Take away the cause, and the effect ceases.
- Cervantes

Like good weed prevention, a countermeasure prevents problems from ever taking root in a process. A good counter-measure not only eliminates the root cause but also prevents other weeds from growing.

Defining Counter-measures

1. Transfer the problem statement from step 2 and the root causes from step 3.
2. For each root cause, identify one to three broad countermeasures (what to do).
3. Rank the effectiveness of each countermeasure (Low, Medium, or High)
4. Identify the specific actions (how to do it) for implementing each countermeasure
5. Rank the feasibility (time, cost) of each specific action (Low, Medium, or High).
6. Decide which specific actions to implement.

Six Sigma Improvement
Step 3 - Prevent The Problem

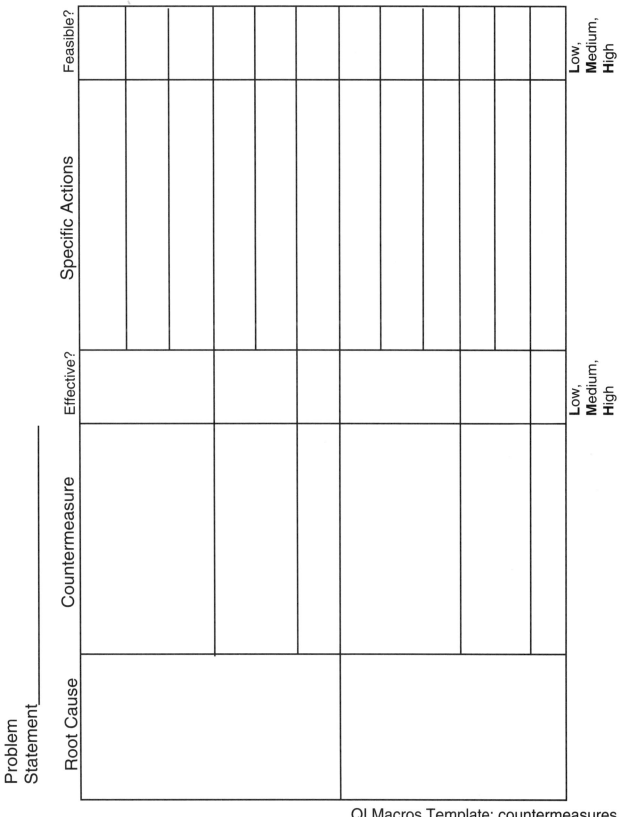

Problem Statement	Root Cause	Countermeasure	Effective? Low, Medium, High	Specific Actions	Feasible? Low, Medium, High

QI Macros Template: countermeasures

Six Sigma Improvement
Step 3 - Prevent The Problem

Purpose

Verify that the problem and its root causes have been reduced

Action should culminate in wisdom.
- Bhagavadgita

To ensure that the improvements take hold, we continue to monitor the measurements (CTQs). Both the line graph and pareto chart will improve if the countermeasures have been successful.

Verify Results

1. Verify that the indicators (CTQs) used in step one have decreased to the target or below.

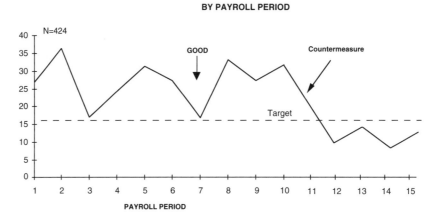

EMPLOYEE PAYCHECK ERRORS
BY PAYROLL PERIOD

2. Verify that the major contributor identified in the Pareto chart in step one has been reduced by comparing before and after pareto charts.

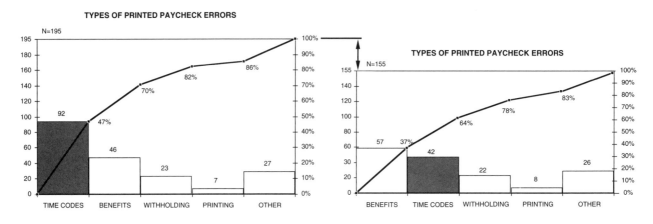

TYPES OF PRINTED PAYCHECK ERRORS

TYPES OF PRINTED PAYCHECK ERRORS

Six Sigma Improvement
Step 3 - Prevent The Problem

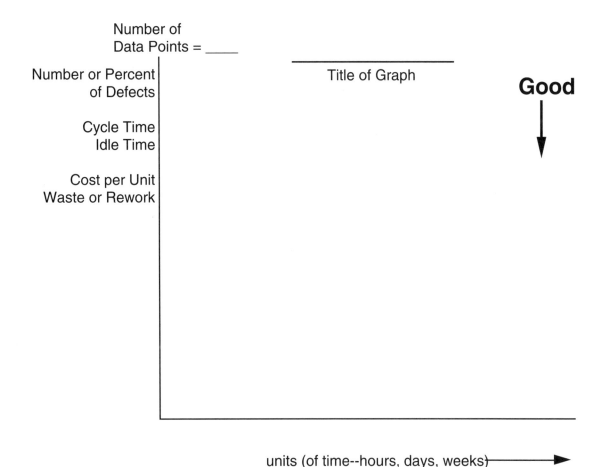

Number of
Data Points = _____

Number or Percent
of Defects

Cycle Time
Idle Time

Cost per Unit
Waste or Rework

_____
Title of Graph

Good
↓

units (of time--hours, days, weeks) →

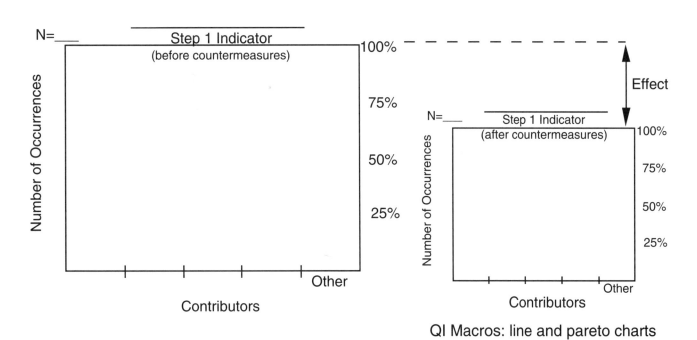

N=___

_____
Step 1 Indicator
(before countermeasures)

Number of Occurrences

100%

75%

50%

25%

Contributors

Other

Effect

N=___

_____
Step 1 Indicator
(after countermeasures)

Number of Occurrences

100%

75%

50%

25%

Contributors

Other

QI Macros: line and pareto charts

Six Sigma Simplified

Six Sigma Improvement
Step 4 - Sustain The Improvement

Purpose

Prevent the problem and its root causes
from coming back

*None will improve
your lot, If you
yourselves do not.
- Bertolt Brecht*

Like crops in a garden, most improvements will require a careful plan to ensure they take root and flourish in other gardens. To transplant these new improvements into other gardens will require a stabilization plan.

Lock in the Gains

ACTION			

Action Plan

WHAT? (Changes)	HOW? (Action)	WHO?	WHEN? Start　Complete	MEASURE? (Results)
People	Training			
Process	Define system and measures Implement Monitor			
Machines (Computers, vehicles, etc.)				
Materials (Forms & Supplies)				
Environ-ment				
Replicate	Identify areas for replication Initiate replication			

QI Macros Template: action

Six Sigma Improvement
Step 4 - Multiply The Gains

Purpose	To increase the return on investment from each improvement effort.

Nothing succeeds like success.
  Alexandre Dumas

To ensure that we get the maximum benefit from having solved this problem, we have to get this improvement into the hands of all the other people who could use it.

Identify Places to Increase the Gains

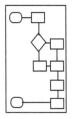

1. Brainstorm a list of potential clients for the improvement. Any group or individual that shares a similar customer, product, or service that could benefit from the improvement.
2. Select the key groups for replication.
3. Forward the process (flowchart and indicators) to the groups targeted for replication.
4. Follow up to ensure that the improvements have been implemented. Replicate any additional enhancements that have been made by these other groups.

WHERE? Where will this process be useful?	WHAT? What needs to be done to initiate?	HOW? How will the process be replicated?	WHO? Who owns the replication?	WHEN? Start	Complete
		Adopt process Adapt process to fit Incorporate existing improvements			

   Six Sigma Simplified

A Six Sigma Case Study

Reducing Computer Downtime

One Baby Bell reduced computer downtime by 74% in just six months using Six Sigma. The next two pages show the actual improvement story.

Define and Measure The Problem

At the beginning, there were 100,000 "seat" minutes of outage per week. Since there were 9,000 service representatives, that means only 11 minutes of outage per week per person, but all totalled, it meant the loss of 1667 hours, 208 person days, or five person weeks. In other words, it was the equivalent of having five service reps unavailable.

Target:

The VP of Operations set a goal of reducing this by 50% which caused a lot of grumbling, but on analysis, they found that 39% of the downtime was caused by the server software, 28% was caused by application software, and 27% server hardware.

Analyze and Improve the Problem

Multiple improvement teams tackled each of these areas. Root cause analysis and verification determined that password file corruption, faulty hardware boards, processes, and one application accounted for most of the failures.

Prevent The Problem

Multiple countermeasures were implemented including up-grades to the operating system in over 600 servers to prevent password file corruption and other problems.

Check Results

In less than six months they had exceeded the goal by achieving a 74% reduction.

Sustain The Improvements (Control)

A system was implemented to monitor and manage outages for both immediate and long-term improvement.

THE SIX SIGMA STORY

Problem-Solving Made Easy

DEFINE THE PROBLEM (Why do I think I have a problem?)

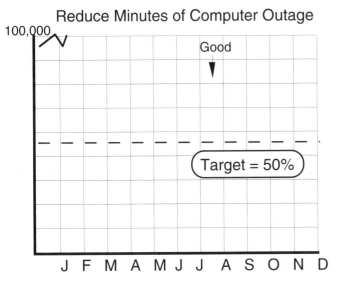

Reduce Minutes of Computer Outage

Good

Target = 50%

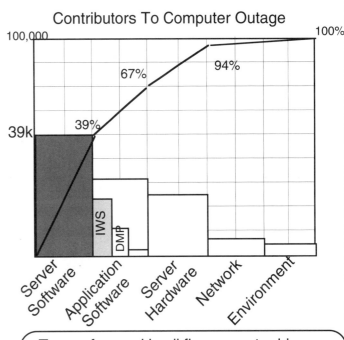

Contributors To Computer Outage

Teams focused in all five areas to drive 50% reductions in outages

ANALYZE THE PROBLEM (What are the causes of the problem?) Cause and Effect

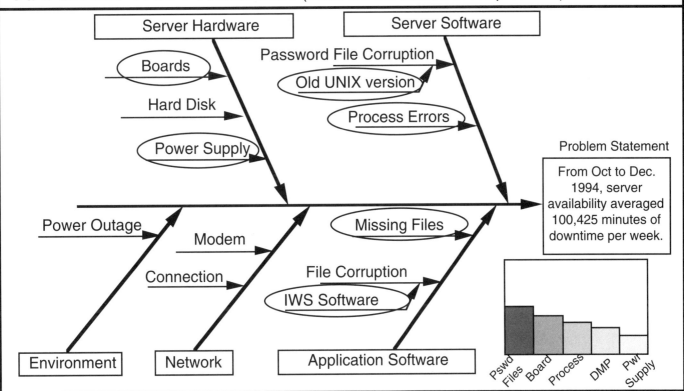

Server Hardware
- Boards
- Hard Disk
- Power Supply

Server Software
- Password File Corruption
- Old UNIX version
- Process Errors

Power Outage
Modem
Connection

Environment
Network

Missing Files
File Corruption
IWS Software

Application Software

Problem Statement

From Oct to Dec. 1994, server availability averaged 100,425 minutes of downtime per week.

PREVENT THE PROBLEM (What steps will correct the problem?)

Root Causes	Countermeasures	Effectiveness (H-M-L)	Specific Actions	Feasibility (H-M-L)
Corrupted Password Files	Upgrade UNIX OS to 5.3	H	Develop and implement installation plan across server environment	H
Multiple other Root causes and countermeasures where implemented				

CHECK RESULTS (Is the suggested solution working?)

Reduce Minutes of Computer Outage

100,000

Good

Target = 50%

J F M A M J J A S O N D

Contributors To Computer Outage

100,000   100%

39%

Server Software
Application Software
Server Hardware
Network
Environment

79% Reduction

20,900   100%

Environment
Server Software
Application Software
Server Hardware
Network

LOCK IN THE IMPROVEMENTS (How do we standardize and replicate it?)

Service Results Management

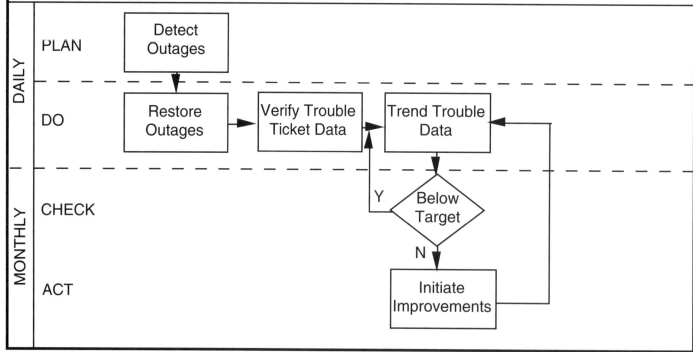

DAILY

PLAN — Detect Outages

DO — Restore Outages → Verify Trouble Ticket Data → Trend Trouble Data

MONTHLY

CHECK — Below Target — Y

ACT — Initiate Improvements — N

The Cost Of Poor Quality

Failure Inspection & Prevention

Flops are part of life's menu.
  Rosalind Russell

Any man can make mistakes, but only an idiot persists in his error.
  Cicero

Perfection has one grave defect: it is apt to be dull.
  Somerset Maugham

Many people worry about how much Six Sigma will cost. J. M. Juran suggests the following way of thinking about the costs of quality.

1. If you don't do anything to ensure a quality product, the cost of <u>failures</u> will be too high. They require either <u>rework</u> (e.g., getting a car fixed under warranty) or <u>waste</u> (e.g., food spoilage in a restaurant).

2. Many companies, in a knee-jerk reaction to these failures institute extensive <u>inspection</u> efforts to catch defective products or services before they reach the customer. Again, this requires significant <u>rework</u> and <u>waste</u>. In the worst cases, half the people are involved in inspection and defect removal.

3. Six Sigma companies, on the other hand, focus on <u>preventing</u> defects. If no one puts defects in, then no one has to find them or fix them. This frees everyone to focus on meeting the needs of customers instead of fixing their complaints.

Most companies prefer firefighting to fire prevention. They simply don't do enough process improvement to prevent the waste and rework costs associated with inspection and failure. Your goal should be to find the optimum balance between prevention, inspection, and failure. Remember, less than 4% of the business causes over 50% of the failures. As you move toward six sigma, total costs will decline even more.

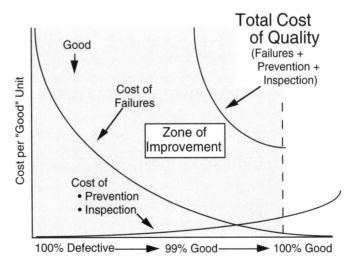

Sustain The Improvement (Control)

Statistical Process Control

SPC deals with the ongoing work of an organization. You have internal customers who receive your products or services. By identifying your customers and their needs, you can establish specifications and targets for your work processes and then define measurements to ensure that you can deliver what the customer requires. Continual monitoring will let you know how well you are satisfying your customers and where improvement of your processes is required. SPC helps you:

Benefits

- Achieve consistency in daily work and improved results
- Clarify contributions toward achieving customer satisfaction
- Systematically improve and control your processes
- Maintain the gains achieved through improvement projects
- Identify processes for Six Sigma Improvement
- Provide focus to problem-solving teams
- Sustain the gains from improvement teams
- Assist in training employees
- Multiply the gains from one system to other similar work processes
- Increase employee understanding of what is expected
- Increase communication in the work place

Key Tools

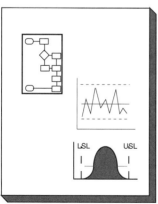

There are <u>three key tools</u> in the SPC process:

- <u>Flowcharts</u> - to define the process flow

- <u>Control charts</u> - to measure the <u>stability</u> of the process

- <u>Histogram</u> - to measure the <u>capability</u> of the process

With these three tools you can monitor, sustain, and control virtually any process.

Sustain The Improvement (Control)

Process Management

There is always a best way of doing everything.
-Emerson

Before we can find better, faster, and cheaper ways of serving customers, we first have to define and stabilize the way of doing business. Making existing processes predictable and capable of meeting customer requirements follows the FISH process– Focus, Improve, Sustain, and Honor.

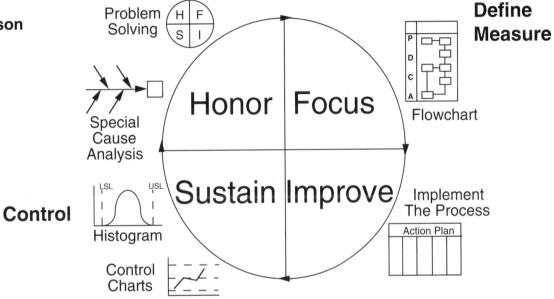

Problem Solving

Special Cause Analysis

Control

Histogram

Control Charts

Honor | Focus

Sustain | Improve

Define Measure

Flowchart

Implement The Process

Action Plan

Process

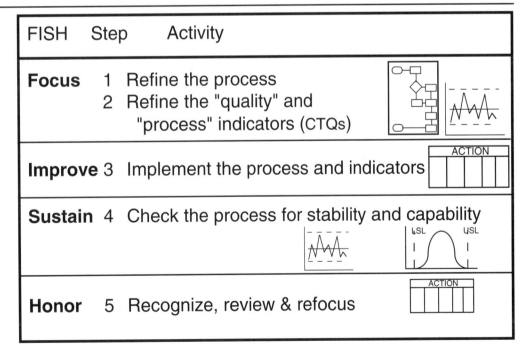

FISH	Step	Activity
Focus	1 2	Refine the process Refine the "quality" and "process" indicators (CTQs)
Improve	3	Implement the process and indicators
Sustain	4	Check the process for stability and capability
Honor	5	Recognize, review & refocus

Sustain The Improvement
Refine The Process

Monitor and Sustain
New Levels of Performance in
Mission Critical Systems

What is the New Process?

1. Refine the Process

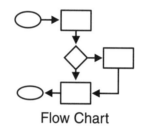

Flow Chart

Is the Process Stable and Predictable?

2. Analyze Stability

Control Charts
(Stability)

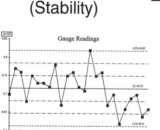

Attribute (defects)	Variable (time, length, weight, temp)
np, p	XmR
c, u	XbarR
	XbarS

Does the Process Meet Customer Expectations?

3. Analyze Capability

Histogram
(Capability)

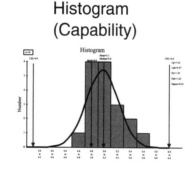

Sustain The Improvement
Refine The Process

Define the improved process as a starting point for stabilization

Flowchart Symbols

A flowchart uses a few simple symbols to show the flow of a process. The symbols are:

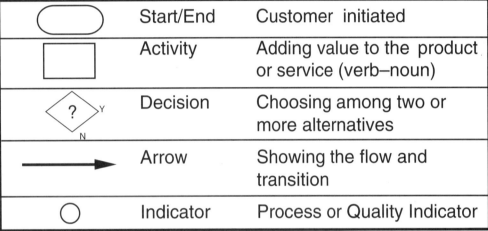

Start/End	Customer initiated
Activity	Adding value to the product or service (verb–noun)
Decision	Choosing among two or more alternatives
Arrow	Showing the flow and transition
Indicator	Process or Quality Indicator

The unified process of drawing and shooting was divided into sections: grasping the bow, nocking the arrow, raising the bow, drawing and remaining at the point of highest tension, loosing the shot.

- Eugen Herrigel

Instead of writing directly on the flowchart, use small Post-it™ notes for both the decisions and activities. This way, the process will remain easy to change until you have it clearly and totally defined. Limit the number of decisions and activities per page. Move detailed subprocesses onto additional pages.

Across the **top** of the flowchart list every person or department that helps deliver the product or service. Along the **left-hand side**, list the major steps in your process: planning, doing, checking, and acting to improve. Even going to the grocery store involves creating a list (plan), getting the groceries (do), checking the list, and acting to get any forgotten item.

Process indicators measure performance <u>during</u> the process. They help find and fix problems before the customer is affected. Put them at critical hand-offs between functions and decision points-especially ones that require error correction.

Quality (CTQ) indicators, measured <u>after</u> delivery, track customer satisfaction with timeliness, accuracy, and value.

Process Indicators

Handoffs

Decisions

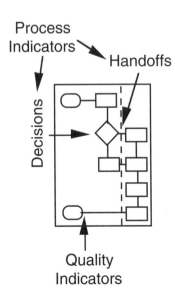

Quality Indicators

Check Stability
Sampling

Purpose	Minimize the cost of collecting the data.

Sampling

By a small sample may we judge the whole piece.
  - Cervantes

To begin managing a process, you will need a minimum of 20 data points for each indicator. To collect data cost effectively, you will have to understand the basic concepts of sampling. If you are only producing ten widgets a day, then it is fairly easy to look at all of them (the *total population* of created widgets). If you produce 100,000 widgets a day, however, you will want to look at a small sample and *draw conclusions* about the entire population from the sample:

Lot or Total Population

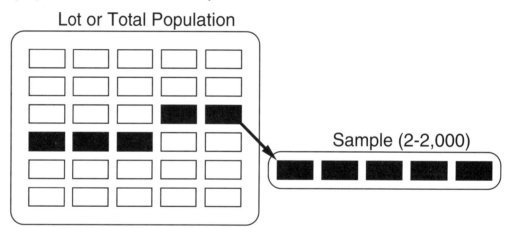

Sample (2-2,000)

In the population, if there is a . . .	then . . .
large number that are measured	
manually	take a sample
mechanically	use the total population
small number	use the total population

Sample Size

When samples are taken, they should be the same size: If you check five widgets in this sample, then you will want to check five widgets *every* time you sample. If you use the total population, it can vary from period to period or be a constant size. In general, the sample size will vary based on: the acceptable level of quality desired, the size of the "lot" you're inspecting, the type of sampling done–single, double, multiple, and the level of inspection. Higher quality requires larger samples.

QI Macros: Sample Size Calculator

Stabilize the Process
Understanding Capability

Capability

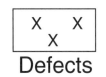

Defects

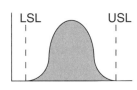

A **capable** process meets the customer's requirements 100% of the time. The upper (USL) and lower (LSL) specification limits are determined from the customer's requirements. The goal of every process is to kick a football through the goal posts *every time*.

The capability of **counted** (i.e., attribute) data like defects–indivisible integers only– is zero defects. Customers hate defects–outages (USL = LSL = 0).

The capability of **measured** (i.e., variable) data like time, money, age, length, width, and weight. is determined using the customer's specifications and a histogram (QI Macros histogram macro).

← Length →

Weight | Height

Time

Cost

$

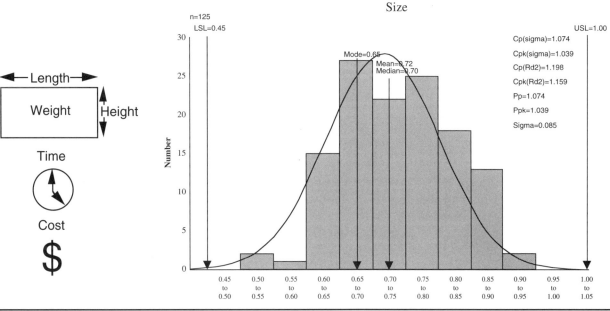

Size

n=125
LSL=0.45

USL=1.00

Mode=0.65
Mean=0.72
Median=0.70

Cp(sigma)=1.074
Cpk(sigma)=1.039
Cp(Rd2)=1.198
Cpk(Rd2)=1.159
Pp=1.074
Ppk=1.039
Sigma=0.085

Problem Solving

Capable
=
Meets Customer Requirements 100% of the Time

Is the process capable? If not, what improvement activities are required to make the process both stable and capable?

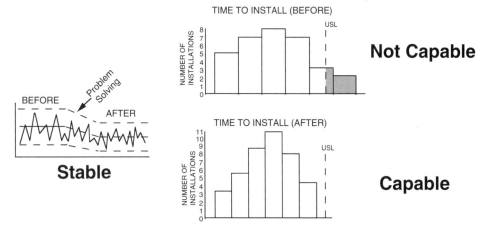

TIME TO INSTALL (BEFORE)

Not Capable

Stable

TIME TO INSTALL (AFTER)

Capable

Stabilize the Process
Understanding Capability

Goal Post vs Target

Traditional thinking took a "goal post" attitude toward process capability. When the customer defines an upper and a lower specification limit for a product or service-whether it's the diameter of a piston or the time in line at a fast food restaurant, all points within the two limits are considered "good." But Taguchi suggested that there is a loss incurred by society as these products and services move away from their target value. This cost increases exponentially with distance from the target value:

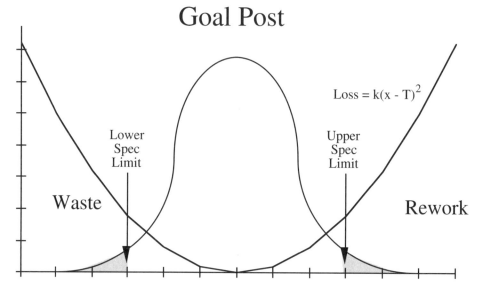

Goal Post

$$Loss = k(x - T)^2$$

Lower Spec Limit

Upper Spec Limit

Waste

Rework

Target thinking encourages minimization of variation, with a resulting savings based on Taguchi's "loss function."

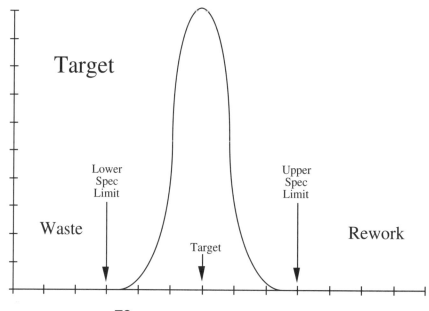

Target

Lower Spec Limit

Upper Spec Limit

Waste

Target

Rework

Six Sigma Simplified

Stabilize the Process
Understanding Capability

Is the process capable? Cp, the process capability index, evaluates the 6σ range of the variation within the process. Cp doesn't care if the process is centered over the target or is off-center, all it cares about is whether or not the data points would fit within the range of the upper and lower specification limits.

Cp

$Cp=(USL-LSL)/6\sigma$ – Capability index without centering

where σ is estimated by $\bar{R}/d_2$ when the process is *statistically stable.*
$\bar{R}$ is the average of the ranges in samples
d_2 is a constant based on the sample size.

Cpk

Cpk, on the other hand, accounts for process centering.

$Cpk=$ Minimum of $(USL-\bar{\bar{X}})/3\sigma$ or $(\bar{\bar{X}}-LSL)/3\sigma$

Capable
Cp≥1, Cpk≥1

When Cp and Cpk are greater than 1.0, the process is capable. In the example below, $Cp_{Left}=Cp_{Right}$, while $Cpk_{Left} > Cpk_{Right}$, because of process centering.

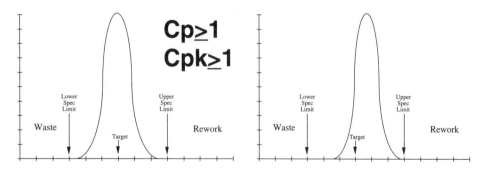

A Cpk value less than zero indicates that most of the points fall outside the specification limits. Note that Cp, in this example is greater than 1.

Conversion Chart	
Cpk	**Sigma**
1.0	3 Sigma
1.33	4 Sigma
1.66	5 Sigma
2.0	6 Sigma

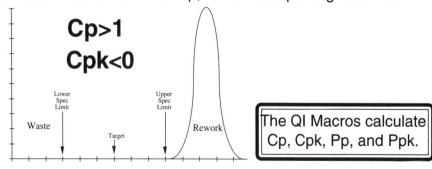

The QI Macros calculate Cp, Cpk, Pp, and Ppk.

Understanding Standard Deviation and Control Charts

Many people ask: "Why aren't my upper and lower control limits (UCL, LCL) calculated as: $\mu \pm 3^*\sigma$ (where μ is the mean and σ is the standard deviation)?"

To answer this question, you have to understand some key principles and underlying statistics: variation, standard deviation, sampling and populations.

Variance

Variance (σ^2) is the average of the square of the **distance between each point in a total population (N) and the mean** (μ).

$$\sigma^2 = \frac{\sum_{i=1}^{N}(x_i - \mu)^2}{N}$$

Same Mean

Different Standard Deviations

If your data is spread over a wider range, you have a higher variance and standard deviation. If the data is centered around the average, you have a smaller variance and standard deviation.

Standard Deviation

Standard deviation (σ) is the square root of the variance (σ^2):

$$\sigma = \sqrt{\sigma^2}$$

And it can be *estimated* using the average range (R):

$$\hat{\sigma} = \overline{R} / d_2$$

Sampling

Sampling: Early users of SPC found that it cost too much to evaluate every item in the <u>total population</u>. To reduce the cost of measuring everything, they had to find a way to evaluate a **small sample** and make inferences from it about the **total population**.

Understanding Standard Deviation and Control Charts

μ is the mean of the total population

σ is the standard deviation of the total population

Understanding Control Chart Limits: Ask yourself this question: "If a simple formula using the mean and standard deviation would work, *why are there so many different control charts?*" Short answer: to save money by measuring small samples, not the entire population.

When using small samples or varying populations the simple formula using the mean and standard deviation just doesn't work, because **you don't know the μ or σ of the *total population*, only your sample**. So why are there so many control charts? Because:

Estimate μ and σ using data from your sample

You have to *estimate* μ and σ using the average and range of your samples. The formulas to do this vary depending on the type of data (variable or attribute) and the sample size. Each control chart's formulas are designed for these varying conditions.

In variable charts, the XmR uses a sample size of 1, XbarR (2-10) and XbarS (11-25). These small samples may be taken from lots of 1,000 or more. In attribute charts, the c and np chart use small samples and "fixed" populations; the u and p charts use varying populations. So, you have to adjust the formulas to compensate for the varying samples and populations.

To reduce the cost of inspection at Western Electric in the 1930s, Dr. Walter S. Shewhart developed a set of formulas and constants to compensate for these variations in sample size and population. That's why they are sometimes called Shewhart Control Charts. You can find these in *any* book on statistical process control (e.g., *Introduction to Statistical Process Control*, Montgomery, Wiley, 2001, pgs 207-265).

So stop worrying about the formulas.
Start monitoring your process using the charts.

Track the Process Indicators

Process Indicators	The measurements of customer requirements usually occur after the end product or service is delivered. To ensure that customers get what they want, we have to set up a system of early warning indicators that will predict whether or not the process will deliver what the customers want. Like the quality indicators, these predictive indicators will need to measure defects, time, and cost <u>inside the process</u>.

Where to Measure

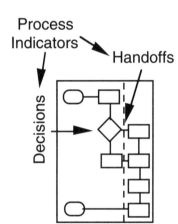

Process Indicators → Handoffs

Decisions →

Often, the easiest points to measure:

• **process indicators** are at the key handoffs (to measure time or missed commitments) or decision points (to measure defects and rework). If, for example, you were trying to <u>predict</u> how long it would take to get to work, the number of red lights or average highway speed could <u>predict</u> the total commute time.

• **quality (CTQ) indicators** (e.g., total commute time) <u>after</u> the product or service has been delivered. Looking back at the main flowchart, at what points could you most easily take measurements that would predict whether the process will be able to deliver what the customers want?

Examples

"Quality" CTQ Indicator	"Process" Early Warning Indicator
Percent defective	Amount of rework per step Number of defects per step
Missed Commitments	Time per process step Delay (idle and rework time)
Value	Cost of waste and rework
Paycheck errors	Timesheet errors % timesheets late
Appliance installation time	Old appliance removal time
Cost of food spoilage	Number of customers Perishable food ordered

Track the Process Indicators

Process Indicators

Number of
Data Points = _____

Title _____

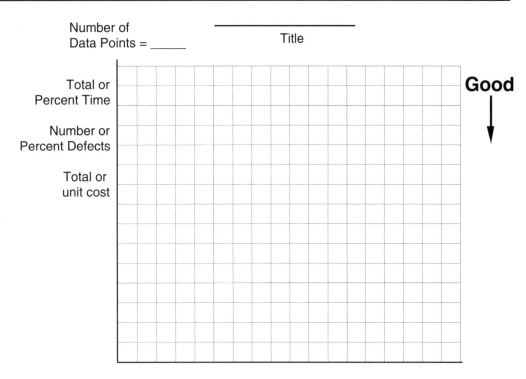

Total or
Percent Time

Number or
Percent Defects

Total or
unit cost

Good
↓

units (of time--hour, day, week, etc.)

Number of
Data Points = _____

Title _____

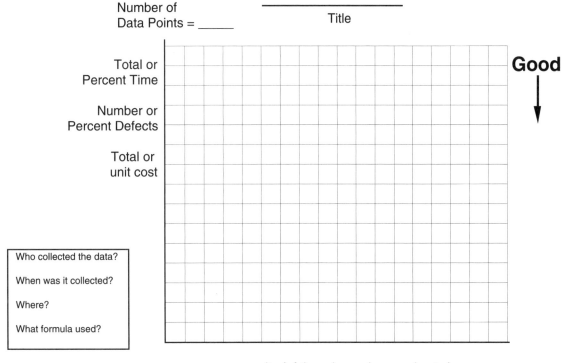

Total or
Percent Time

Number or
Percent Defects

Total or
unit cost

Good
↓

Who collected the data?

When was it collected?

Where?

What formula used?

units (of time--hour, day, week, etc.)

Stabilize the Process
Understanding Stability

Stability

A stable process produces <u>predictable results consistently</u>. Stability can be easily determined from control charts. The upper (UCL) and lower control limit (LCL) are <u>calculated</u> from the data.

Example

How long does it take you to commute to work each morning?

**Stable
=
Predictable**

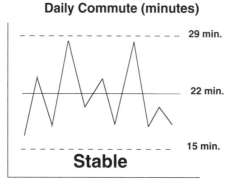

Daily Commute (minutes)
29 min.
22 min.
15 min.
Stable

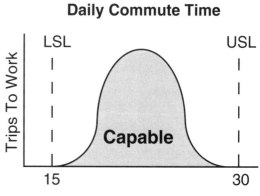

Daily Commute Time
LSL   USL
Capable
15   30

Your Requirements
1. Get to work in 30 minutes or less.
2. Get to work safely (no faster than 15 minutes).

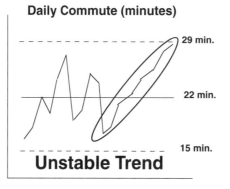

Daily Commute (minutes)
29 min.
22 min.
15 min.
Unstable Trend

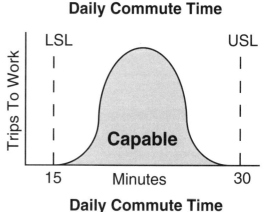

Daily Commute Time
LSL   USL
Capable
15   Minutes   30

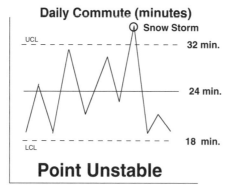

Daily Commute (minutes)
Snow Storm
UCL   32 min.
24 min.
18 min.
LCL
Point Unstable

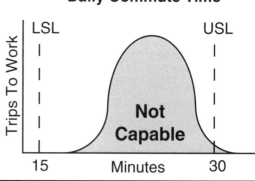

Daily Commute Time
LSL   USL
Not Capable
15   Minutes   30

Stability and Capability

A process does not have to be stable to be capable of meeting the customer's requirements. Similarly, a stable process is not necessarily capable. A predictable process must be both stable <u>and</u> capable. Interpreting stability with control charts and capability with histograms will be discussed in more detail on the following pages.

Check Stability
Interpreting The Indicators

Purpose	Verify that the process system is stable and can predictably meet customer requirements

Variation

You cannot step twice into the same river.

  Heraclitus

A stable process produces <u>predictable results</u>. Understanding variation helps us learn how to predict the performance of any process. To ensure that the process is stable (i.e., predictable) we need to develop "run" or "control" charts of our indicators.

How can you tell if a process is stable? Processes are never perfect. *Common* and *special causes* of variation make the process perform differently in different situations. Getting to school or work takes varying amounts of time because of traffic or transportation delays. These are <u>common cause</u>s of variation; they exist every day. A blizzard, a traffic accident, a chemical spill, or other freak occurrence that causes major delays would be a <u>special cause</u> of variation.

In the 1920s, Dr. Shewhart, at Bell Labs, developed ways to evaluate whether the data on a line graph is common cause or special cause variation. Using 20-30 data points, you can determine how stable and predictable the process is. Using simple equations, software can calculate the average (center line), and the upper and lower "control limits" from the data. 99% of all *expected* (i.e., common cause variation) should lie between these two limits. Control limits are not to be confused with specification limits. Specification limits are defined by the customer. Control limits show what the process can deliver.

Example

Your Requirements:
1. Get to work fast!
2. Get to work safely.

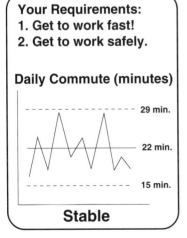

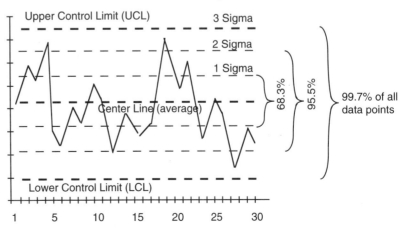

Check Stability
Interpreting The Indicators

Special Cause Variation	Processes that are "out of control" need to be stabilized before they can be improved using the problem-solving process. Special causes require immediate cause-effect analysis to eliminate the special cause of variation.
Evaluating Stability	The following diagram will help you evaluate stability in any control chart. Unstable conditions can be any of the following:

Daily Commute (minutes)

Snow Storm
29 min.
22 min.
15 min.

Point Unstable

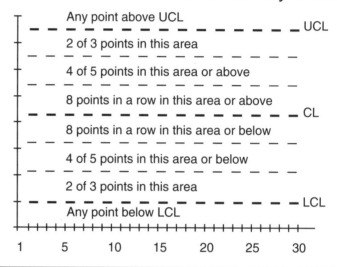

Any point above UCL — UCL
2 of 3 points in this area
4 of 5 points in this area or above
8 points in a row in this area or above — CL
8 points in a row in this area or below
4 of 5 points in this area or below
2 of 3 points in this area
Any point below LCL — LCL

1   5   10   15   20   25   30

Points and Runs	Any point outside the upper or lower control limits is a clear example of a special cause. The other forms of special cause variation are called "runs." Trends, cycling up and down, or "hugging" the center line or limits are special forms of a run.

Daily Commute (minutes)

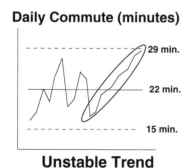

29 min.
22 min.
15 min.

Unstable Trend

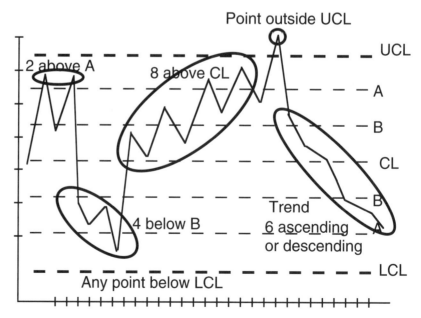

Point outside UCL
UCL
2 above A
8 above CL
A
B
CL
4 below B
Trend
6 ascending
or descending
B
A
Any point below LCL
LCL

The QI Macros
analyze stability
using these rules.

Check Stability
Choosing a Chart

Types of Charts

Next, you have to know what to collect about each widget. Do you need to know: how long it takes to deliver a product or service, the number of defects per product, or the cost of waste or rework? Time, cost, length, and weight are known as *variable* data. Counting the number of defects or defective items gives *attribute* data. The type of data (attribute or variable) and the size of the sample taken (1, 2-10, or total) will determine the type of graph used to measure the process.

Choosing a Chart

Type of data	Sample Size			
	1	Same Size	Varies	
Attribute data X = 1 Defective		**np** (2-total)	**p** (total)	
X X X = 3 Defects	**c**		**u** (total)	
Variable data Length Weight Height Time Cost $	**XmR**	**XR XS** (size 2-25)	**XS**	
Y Axis	Number	Number	Percent	

Drawing the Chart

Regardless of sample size, each of these charts can be drawn as a *line graph.* **Tip:** If the math seems scary, start with line graphs or get the QI Macros for Microsoft® Excel.

- The **X axis** (horizontal) shows how often the data is collected (daily, hourly, weekly, periodically).
- The **Y axis** (vertical) shows:
  - the number or percent defective (c, np, p, u)
  - the time, cost, length, weight, etc. (XR charts)

Then, based on the type of data and sample size, you can calculate the upper and lower control limits (UCL, LCL) and center line (CL) that will make it possible to evaluate process stability. The next few pages show how to calculate and interpret the limits.

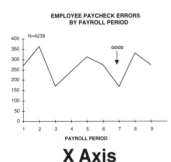

X Axis

Check Stability
Choosing a Chart

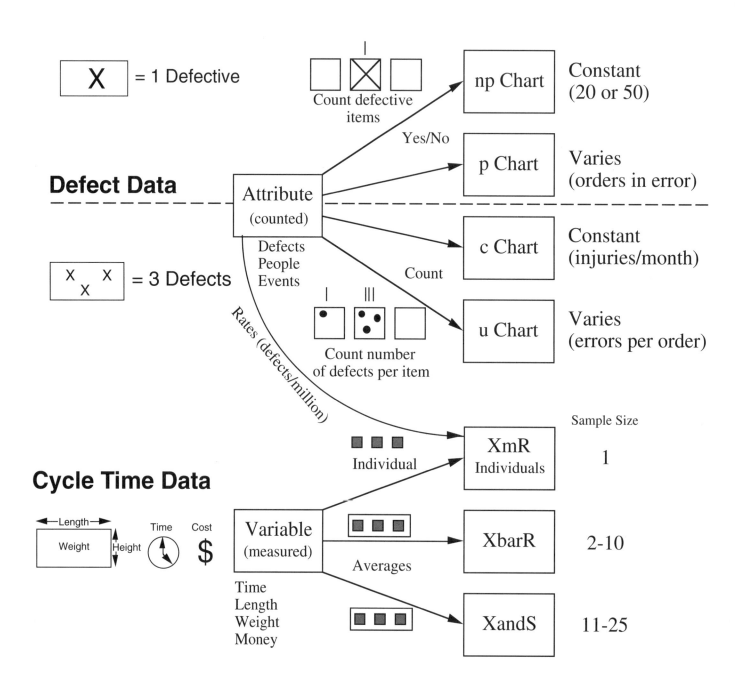

| X | = 1 Defective |

Count defective items

np Chart — Constant (20 or 50)

Defect Data

Yes/No

p Chart — Varies (orders in error)

| X X / X | = 3 Defects |

Attribute (counted)

Defects
People
Events

c Chart — Constant (injuries/month)

Count

Count number of defects per item

u Chart — Varies (errors per order)

Rates (defects/million)

Sample Size

XmR Individuals — 1

Individual

Cycle Time Data

Length, Weight, Height, Time, Cost $

Variable (measured)

XbarR — 2-10

Time
Length
Weight
Money

Averages

XandS — 11-25

Step 4 - Check Stability
np and p charts

p and np Charts
(Attribute data)

Defective

The p and np charts will help you evaluate process stability when counting the number or fraction <u>defective</u>. Examples might include: the number of defective circuit boards, meals in a restaurant, teller interactions in a bank, invoices, or bills.

The np chart is useful when it's easy to count the number of defective items and the sample size is always the same. The p chart is used when the sample size varies: the total number of circuit boards, meals, or bills delivered varies from one sampling period to the next. In the p chart below, the number of defective paychecks varies with the number of employees in each pay period.

Paychecks - Fraction Defective

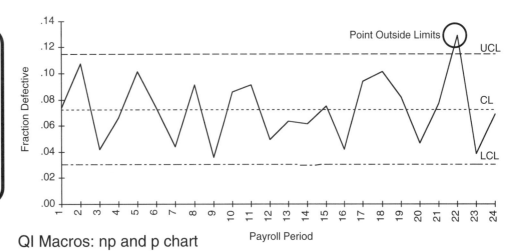

QI Macros: np and p chart

Stability

Given this information, we would want to investigate why the 22nd payroll period was "out of control." Otherwise, this chart, and therefore this process, look stable.

Capability

A fully capable process delivers <u>zero defects</u>. Although this may be difficult to achieve, it should still be our goal. Once we resolve the out-of-control point, we could use the problem solving process to begin to eliminate the common causes of defective paychecks. What are the most common types of paycheck errors? Why do they occur? What are the root causes of these paycheck errors?

Step 4 - Check Stability
c and u charts

c and u Charts
(Attribute data)

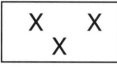

Defects

The c and u charts will help you evaluate process stability when there can be more than one defect per unit. Examples might include: the number of defective elements on a circuit board, the number of defects in a dining experience–order wrong, food too cold, check wrong, or the number of defects in bank statement, invoice, or bill. This chart is especially useful when you want to know how many defects there are not just how many defective items there are. It's one thing to know how many defective circuit boards, meals, statements, invoices, or bills there are; it is another thing to know how many defects were found in these defective items.

The c chart is useful when it's easy to count the number of defects and the sample size is always the same. The u chart is used when the sample size varies: the number of circuit boards, meals, or bills delivered each day varies. The c chart below shows the number of defects per day in a uniform sample.

To automate all of your control charts using Microsoft® Excel, get the *QI Macros For Excel.* Download a FREE limited demo from: www.qimacros.com

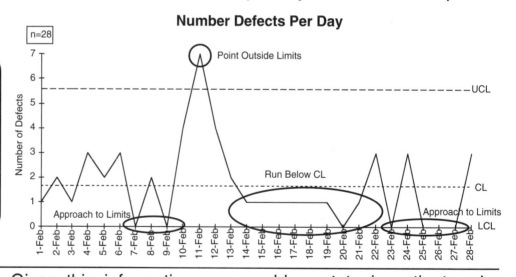

Number Defects Per Day

Stability

Given this information, we would want to investigate why February 11th was "out of control." We would also want to understand why we were able to keep the defects so far below average in the other circled areas. What did we do here that was so successful?

Capability

A fully capable process delivers <u>zero defects</u>.

Download control chart forms from qimacros.com/forms.html

Six Sigma Simplified

Step 4 - Check Stability
X Charts

XR XS Chart
(Variable data Sample Size=5)

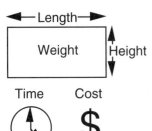

The XR chart can help you evaluate the cycle time for almost any process: making a widget, answering a customer call, seating a customer, delivering a pizza, or servicing an appliance. This chart is especially useful when you do this many times a day. Collecting the data could be expensive if you measured every time you did it. Using a small sample (typically five and as many as 25) you can effectively measure and evaluate the process.

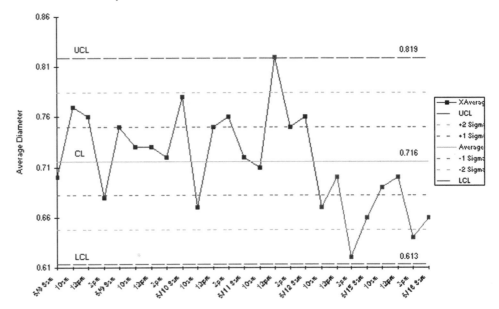

XmR Chart
(Variable Data, Sample Size=1)

The XmR (Individuals and Moving Range) chart can help you evaluate a process when there is only one measurement and they are farther apart: monthly postage expense and so on. The XmR can also be used for ratios (e.g., parts per million).

Calculate, plot, and evaluate the <u>range chart first</u>. If it is "out of control," so is the process. If the range chart looks okay, then calculate, plot, and evaluate the X chart.

Step 4 - Check Stability
Control Chart Formulas

---

p and np
(Attribute data)

p Chart
UCL: $\bar{p} + 3*sqrt(\bar{p}*(1-\bar{p})/n_i)$
CL: $\bar{p} = \sum p_i/\sum n_i$
LCL: $\bar{p} - 3*sqrt(\bar{p}*(1-\bar{p})/n_i)$

np Chart
$n\bar{p} + 3*sqrt(\bar{n}p*(1-\bar{n}p/n))$
$n\bar{p} = \sum np_i/k$
$n\bar{p} - 3*sqrt(\bar{n}p*(1-\bar{n}p/n))$

---

c and u
(Attribute data)

C Chart
UCL: $\bar{c} + 3*sqrt(\bar{c})$
CL: $\bar{c} = \sum c_i/n$
LCL: $\bar{c} - 3*sqrt(\bar{c})$

U Chart
$\bar{u} + 3*sqrt(\bar{u}/n_i)$
$\bar{u} = \sum u_i/\sum n_i$
$\bar{u} - 3*sqrt(\bar{u}/n)$

XmR Chart
(Variable Data, Sample Size=1)

XmR

	R Chart		X Chart
UCL:	$3.268*\bar{R}$		$\bar{X} + 2.660\bar{R}$
CL:	$\bar{R} = \sum R_i/(k-1)$	R=abs($X_i - X_{i-1}$)	$\bar{X} = \sum X_i/k$
LCL:	0		$\bar{X} - 2.660\bar{R}$

i

$\overline{X}R$ Chart
(Variable data Sample Size=2-10) $\overline{X}R$

	R Chart	(For Sample Size=5)	$\overline{X}$ Chart
UCL:	$2.114*\bar{R}$		$\bar{X} + .577*\bar{R}$
CL:	$\bar{R} = \sum R_i/k$	R=Max(X_i)-Min(X_i)	$\bar{\bar{X}} = \sum \bar{X}_i/k$
LCL:	0		$\bar{\bar{X}} - .577*\bar{R}$

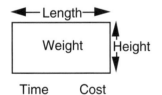

Time   Cost

                                       Six Sigma Simplified

Act To Improve
Special Cause Analysis

Purpose

Improve process stability

If the process is <u>not stable</u>, we can use the Six Sigma problem solving tools, especially the Ishikawa Diagram, to identify the root causes of the instability, remove them, and make the process stable, repeatable, and predictable.

Special Cause Analysis

Every why has a wherefore.
- Shakespeare

1. To identify root causes, use the fishbone or Ishikawa diagram. Put a problem statement about the special cause of variation in the head of the fish and the major causes at the end of the major bones. Major causes include:

   • Processes, machines, materials, measurement, people, environment
   • Steps of a process (step1, step2, etc.)
   • Whatever makes sense

2. Begin with the most likely main cause.

3. For each cause, ask "Why?" up to five times.

4. Circle one-to-five <u>root</u> causes (end of "why" chain)

5. Verify the root causes with data (Pareto, Scatter)

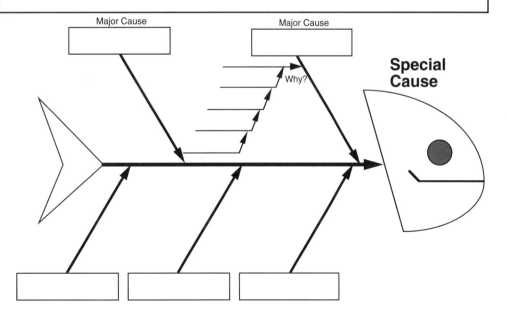

Track Performance
Deploy Measurement Dashboard

Purpose

To visually link targets and measurements throughout the business, and to show progress.

The measurement dashboard links targets and measurements across an organization. The dashboard shows how each group will contribute to the achievement of the overall goal. The dashboard is a tree diagram that contains graphs of each group's performance.

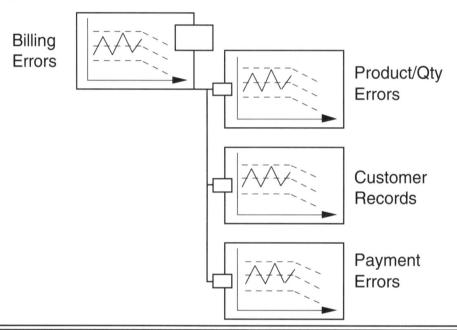

Flag System

FISH	Step	Activity
Focus	1	Identify the gap between current performance and that required for customer satisfaction.
	2	Identify the targets for each group.
Improve	3	Plot the overall improvement graph.
	4	Plot the contributing graphs for each target.
	5	Display and update these graphs monthly.
Sustain	6	Review movement toward targets.
Honor	7	Refocus improvement efforts as required.

Honor Your Progress

Quality Reviews

For Six Sigma to be successful, it needs ongoing, periodic attention to recognize, review, and revise improvement efforts. Reviews conducted by all levels of management will help make the improvement effort visible and elevate its importance in the eyes of employees. It also helps management shift from reactive fire fighting to proactive fire prevention. Here's a suggested review schedule:

- Quarterly   - Presidential Review
- Bimonthly   - Middle Management Review
- Monthly   - Line Management Review

Review Process

Step	Activity
1	Track and review improvement efforts.

Which objectives are. . .	take action to . . .
• on target	recognize participants
• in trouble	assist in achievement
• in jeopardy	refocus or revise

Step	Activity
2	Refocus objectives, teams, and improvement efforts as required.

Recognize and Reward

Improvement efforts require recognition and reward to ensure that they continue. There are two elements to consider when evaluating team performance:

- Results - How did the business improve?
- Process - How well did the team apply Six Sigma?

Refocus and Revise

The original improvement focus, like all business objectives, will need to be adjusted as new information comes to light. Did the indicators (i.e., measurements) truly measure the customer's requirements? Were some of the improvement targets too high? Where some too low and achieved easily? Were some of the means to achieve the targets unfocused or incorrect? If so, then revise and refocus the improvement efforts. Continue this cycle forever: focus the improvement efforts, make improvements, sustain, an honor them.

Design For Six Sigma
Process

When to Use?

When you want to achieve at least 4.5-Sigma when designing new products or redesigning existing products.

While the laser-focused (FISH) improvement process deals in existing products and processes, Design for Six Sigma (DFSS) deals with new or redesigned products. The goal is to design a product and the process to produce it in ways that will achieve at least 4.5 sigma (1000 PPM).

DFSS starts with the Voice of the Customer to determine their requirements and convert them into CTQs (critical to quality measures). These requirements are converted into internal design, parts, process, and production requirements. These internal requirements are compared to internal standards and competitive benchmarks. Along the way you also seek to find and prevent every way that a part or process can fail. Then, various production factors, like time and temperature, are compared to determine the optimal settings for best results.

Process

FISH	Step	Activity
Focus	1	**Use Quality Function Deployment** (QFD) to establish requirements, benchmark the competition, and establish Critical to Quality (CTQs) design requirements.
Improve	2	**Use Pugh Concept Selection Matrix** to choose among design alternatives.
	3	**Use Failure Mode and Effects Analysis** (FMEA) to identify potential problems with products and processes and design methods to prevent failures.
	4	**Use Design of Experiments** (DOE) to create a "robust" design that optimizes key factors in the production process.
	5	**Use Reliability tools** like the block diagram to optimize product and process reliability.
	6.	**Use simulations** to evaluate the design.

Design For Six Sigma
Process

Redesign The Process

To succeed in the turbulent 2000s, you will need both innovation and Six Sigma (improvement). Without paradigm shifts (i.e., innovation) you cannot keep up. Without Six Sigma, you cannot improve on innovations quickly enough to survive. You need both! Joel Barker describes three key players in a paradigm shift:

Paradigm shifters–who discover the new paradigm

Paradigm pioneers–who figure out how to use and continuously improve (e.g., developers of Yahoo–Internet).

Paradigm settlers–who come in when it's "safe."

Innovation and Improvement

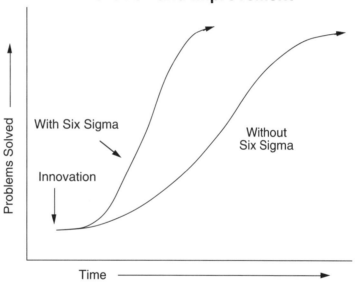

Key Tools

There are <u>three key tools</u> in the DFSS process:

- <u>Process Flowcharts</u> - to define the current and redesigned process

- <u>Matrices</u> - to <u>align</u> the new process with the customer's requirements

- <u>Line Graphs</u> - to measure the performance of the process.

With these three tools you can redesign virtually any process to be tenfold better, faster, and cheaper.

Quality Function Deployment
(Design for Six Sigma)

QFD

Always design a thing by considering it in its next larger context.
Eliel Saarinen

Quality Function Deployment (QFD) recognizes that Six Sigma quality must be integrated into every aspect of a new product, process, or service. Quality cannot be added on or tested in later. QFD seeks to take the customer's requirements (the "Voice of the Customer") and turn them into design requirements that will dramatically improve customer satisfaction while slashing traditional cycle times.

QFD Process

The QFD process is a rigorous planning process to ensure that customer's requirements will be satisfied. It can slash the time required to design new products or services, and it can be used to reengineer business processes.

Phase	Step	Activity
Service	1	Gather the Voice of the Customer through surveys and analysis of customer correspondence and complaints.
	2	Develop and analyze the design requirements (House of Quality).
Delivery	3	Develop a "blueprint" of the delivery process.
Resources	4	Identify the people, process, and technology needed to establish and maintain product and service delivery.
Operations	5	Act to implement process.

QFD House of Quality
(Design for Six Sigma)

Why?

When?

Designing new products and processes to achieve Six Sigma.

How?

1. Service: Gather the Voice of the Customer through surveys and analysis of customer correspondence and complaints. Develop and analyze the design requirements (House of Quality).

2. **Delivery**: Develop a "blueprint" of the delivery process.

3. **Resources:** Identify the people, process, and technology needed to establish and maintain product and service delivery.

4. **Operations**: Act to implement process.

QFD (Quality Function Deployment) is a rigorous planning process to ensure that customer's requirements will be satisfied. It can slash the time required to design new products or services, and it can be used to reengineer business processes.

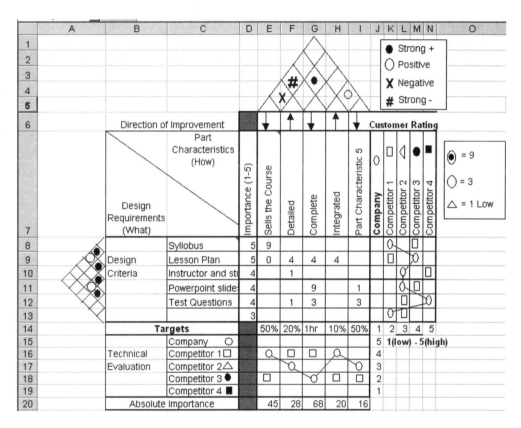

QI Macros Template: QFDhouse.xlt

House of Quality

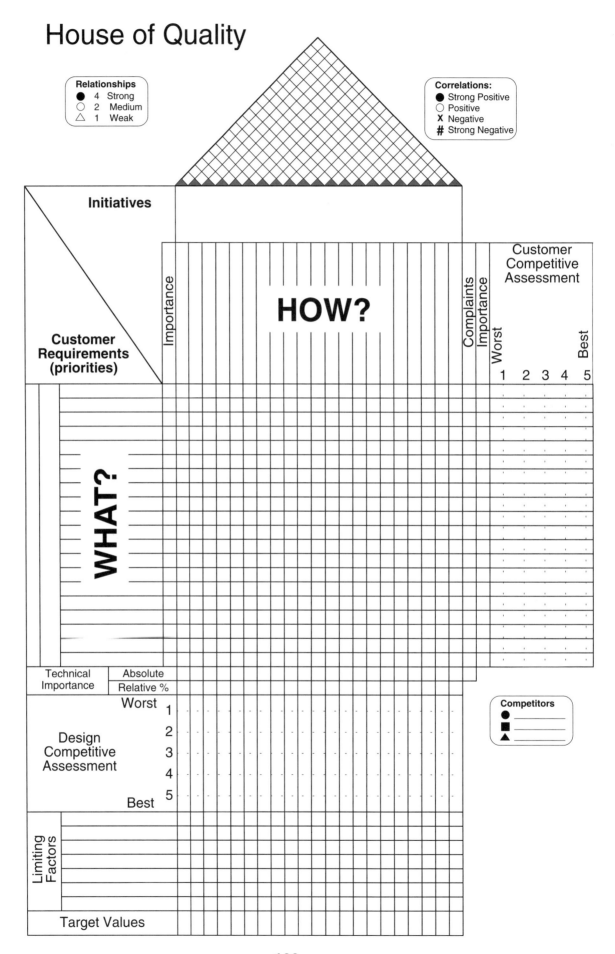

Relationships
- ● 4 Strong
- ○ 2 Medium
- △ 1 Weak

Correlations:
- ● Strong Positive
- ○ Positive
- X Negative
- # Strong Negative

Initiatives

Importance

HOW?

Customer Requirements (priorities)

Complaints Importance

Customer Competitive Assessment

Worst   Best
1 2 3 4 5

WHAT?

| Technical Importance | Absolute |
| | Relative % |

Design Competitive Assessment

Worst 1
2
3
4
Best 5

Competitors
- ● _____
- ■ _____
- ▲ _____

Limiting Factors

Target Values

Design of Experiments
Design for Six Sigma

Purpose	Experiment efficiently to create robust designs

The purpose of DOE is to quickly and efficiently discover the optimum conditions that produce top quality. Trial-and-error is the slowest method of discovering these optimal conditions and usually misses the effects of various interactions. DOE significantly reduces the time and trials necessary to discover the best combination of factors to produce the desired level of quality and robustness.

Design Factors

	A	B	AB
1	-	-	+
2	+	-	-
3	-	+	-
4	+	+	+

Many factors affect the quality of a good or service. In manufacturing, time, temperature, pressure, etc. can all affect the quality and durability of a part or product. There may also be interactions among these various factors that affect product quality and robustness. For example, the amount of time various coats of a car's finish are baked at various temperatures will affect the durability of the paint over time.

DOE can also be used in service industries although it takes a little more thought to determine the factors, their high (+) and low (-) levels, and to quantify their interactions.

DOE Process

DOE Designs
Plackett-Burnam
Full Factorials
22, 23, 24

Taguchi
Screening
L4, L8, L16, etc.

Focus	1. Determine objectives (biggest-smallest, most-least, closest to target), potential causes, and factors (usually 2, 3, or 4 factors).
	2. Select experimental factors, identify potential interactions, and levels (+/-,high/low)
	3. Choose appropriate design (4, 8, or 16 trials) and randomize sequence of trials
Improve	4. Run the experiment
	5. Analyze the data to determine interactions and best factor levels
	6. Verify results
Sustain	7. Implement the optimum factors

Design for Six Sigma
Design of Experiments

Why?

When?

After problem solving to identify plan for implementing changes.

How?

1. Determine objectives, potential causes, and factors (usually 2, 3, or 4 factors).

2. Select experimental factors, identify potential interactions, and levels (+/-,high/low)

3. Choose appropriate design (4, 8, or 16 trials) and randomize sequence of trials

4. Run the experiment

5. Analyze the data to determine interactions and best factor levels

6. Verify results

In the example below, a two factor experiment, we want to evaluate the temperature of a casting die vs the time to pour the material into the die. Two temperatures and two pour times are tested. Four trials that test all four levels are done randomly. There are three sets of trials. While both high temp and time increase the scores (see charts), the interactions show that a high pour time reduces the effect at higher temperatures.

	A	B	C	D	E	F	G	H	I	J
1	Design of Experiments				L4					
2	Factor	Factor Name			Level 1		Level 2			
3	A	Die Temperature			Room temp		200 degrees			
4	B	Pour Time			6 sec		12 sec			
5	AB	Die Temperature X Pour Time								
6										
7	Design	Factors				Trial Responses				
8	Trial	A	B	AB	1	2	3	Average		
9	1	-	-	+	122.3	121.5	121.9	121.90		
10	2	-	+	-	128.5	129	128.2	128.57		
11	3	+	-	-	127.3	127.9	127.8	127.67		
12	4	+	+	+	125.8	125.2	126.2	125.73		
13				Average	125.98	125.90	126.03	125.97		
14		(1)	3	2						
15	Interactions		(2)	1						
16				(3)						
17				Pour Time Low	Pour Time High					
18	Low (-)	125.23	124.78	121.90	128.57					
19	High (+)	126.70	127.15	127.67	125.73					
20										
21	Anova	Factor			df	SS	MS	F	Effect	Contrast
22	Source	Die Temperature			1	6.45	6.45333	37.9608	1.5	8.80
23		Pour Time			1	16.80	16.8033	98.8431	2.4	14.20
24		Die Temperature X Pour Time			1	55.47	55.47	326.294	-4.3	-25.80
25		Error			8	1.36	0.170			
26		Total			11	80.09				

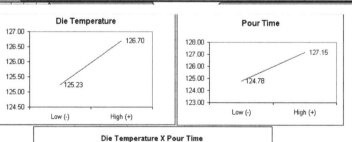

Die Temperature
127.00, 126.70, 126.50, 126.00, 125.50, 125.23, 125.00, 124.50 — Low (-), High (+)

Pour Time
128.00, 127.00, 127.15, 126.00, 125.00, 124.78, 124.00, 123.00 — Low (-), High (+)

Die Temperature X Pour Time
130.00, 128.57, 128.00, 127.67, 126.00, 125.73, 124.00, 122.00, 121.90, 120.00, 118.00 — Low (-), High (+)
Pour Time Low
Pour Time High

Slope of line shows there is an effect caused by both factors.

(Flat line = no effect.)

Optimal solution lies at intersection of "confounding" factors (e.g., higher temp, longer pour time).

QI Macros Template: DOE.xlt

Six Sigma Simplified

Measurement Systems Analysis
Gage R&R

Why?
When?

When you suspect measurement error is contributing to waste, rework, and scrap.

How?

1. Pick 2-3 appraisers

2. Each appraiser measures 10 parts in 2-5 "trials."

3. Put your data into the GageR&R template.

4. Evaluate the results: %R&R measures the appraiser's and gage's contribution to variation. If %R&R<10%, then the measurement system is OK. 10-30% may be OK.

Measurement error can be one of the root causes of waste and rework, especially in manufacturing. Gage Repeatability and Reproducibility (GR&R) helps identify and minimize measurement error.

There are four components of variation 1) the person measuring (Reproducibility: AV-appraiser variation), 2) the gage equipment (Repeatability: EV-equipment variation), 3) interaction of appraiser and gage (R&R), and 4) part variation (PV). Part variation should account for most of the variation, not the appraiser or gage!

If repeatability is larger than reproducibility:
1. gage instrument needs maintenance
2. gage needs to be redesigned
3. clamping or location needs to be improved
4. excessive within-part variation

If reproducibility is larger than repeatability:
1. Operator needs to be trained in how to use and read gage
2. Calibrations on gage are not clear
3. Fixture required to help operator use gage consistently.

QI Macros Template: GageR&R.xlt

Six Sigma Implementation Plan

Purpose

Identify who will do what and when

Action will remove the doubt that theory cannot solve.
    Tehyi Hsieh

Implementing Six Sigma will require a careful plan to ensure that it will take root and flourish. Otherwise, it would be like scattering seeds over hardened soil and hoping for the best. First, leadership must take the time to clear the fields and develop a plan that focuses the organization on a few key areas for *Six Sigma*. This requires setting long- and short-term objectives, measures, and targets.

Then, leadership can identify the few core processes that are essential to the organization's success. Using SPC, you will want to define and measure these processes. Some of these processes will be so far out of date and inflexible that only benchmarking or reengineering will close the gap between where you are and where your customers expect you to be in the near future. Problem-solving will quickly move your other processes in line with customer expectations.

Action Planning

ACTION				

A good Six Sigma implementation plan will identify:

• **What** activities to implement
• **How** to do them
• **Who** will do them
• **When** they will be started and completed
• **How** they will be measured

 Six Sigma Simplified

Six Sigma Implementation Plan

ACTION PLAN

WHAT?		HOW? (Specific Action)	WHO?	WHEN? Start	Complete	MEASURE? (Results)
Focus	Gather Voice of the Customer, Business, & Employees					
	Develop Balanced Scorecard					
Improve	Initiate improvement projects • Problem Solving • Core Process • Benchmarking • Reengineering					
Sustain	Track and evaluate indicators					
Honor	Reward teams Review and Refocus targets as appropriate					

Executive Summary

Plan of Action: Implement Six Sigma:

Breakthrough Improvement

- create Six Sigma skills in key employees
- create measurable results during implementation
- transfer the skills of Six Sigma to the initial wave of team members
- transfer ongoing implementation to internal consultant-trainers selected from successful initial teams.

Process:

Implementing Breakthrough Improvement

1. Learn the essence of laser-focused improvement and SPC.

Focus 2. Focus your improvement efforts to achieve six sigma reductions in cycle time, defects, and cost, which translate to dramatic improvements in customer satisfaction, speed, quality, and profitability. 4% of the business creates over 50% of the problems.

Improve 3. Employ the Six Sigma problem solving process and apply it in multiple parallel teams to achieve quantum leaps in improvement.

Sustain 4. Stabilize and sustain the improved processes to ensure continued high performance.

Honor 5. Develop internal consultant-trainers to continue the implementation.

Considerations:

Profit-Stock Price

A one cent increase in profits can add millions of dollars to your stock price.

If every Six Sigma project delivers $250,000 (or 25 million cents) in profit, how many projects do you need?

Number of Shares = 25 million/project

number of projects needed to bump profits a penny.

The statistics are ominous: over half of all TQM efforts failed; the same will be true for Six Sigma. A typical company invests 42 hours per employee per year to develop Green belt skills and 160 hours for Black belt training. At a loaded cost of $100/hr, that means $4000 per Green belt and $15,000 or more for a Black belt. If you have 100 employees, that's $420,000/yr just for training, add another 40 hours for team meetings. With Six Sigma Simplified, employees get 2 hours of Just-In-Time training and 4-6 hours of results-creating experience. When a critical mass—20-30% of the people—have this deep experience with Six Sigma, the change cascades through the company.

Approach:

1. Under NO circumstances should you attempt to train everyone and do everything. As shown on the next page, leaders must focus on the top one, two, or three priorities and develop the first steps of the improvement story. If leaders, guided by skilled consultants, cannot do this, neither can a team.

2. Once you know exactly which problems to solve first, you will know who should be on the root cause analysis team. This team should meet for no more than two days to hammer out the root causes and proposed solutions (i.e., countermeasures).

3. Implementation teams should implement and sustain the process.

Six Sigma Improvement
To Achieve Six Sigma

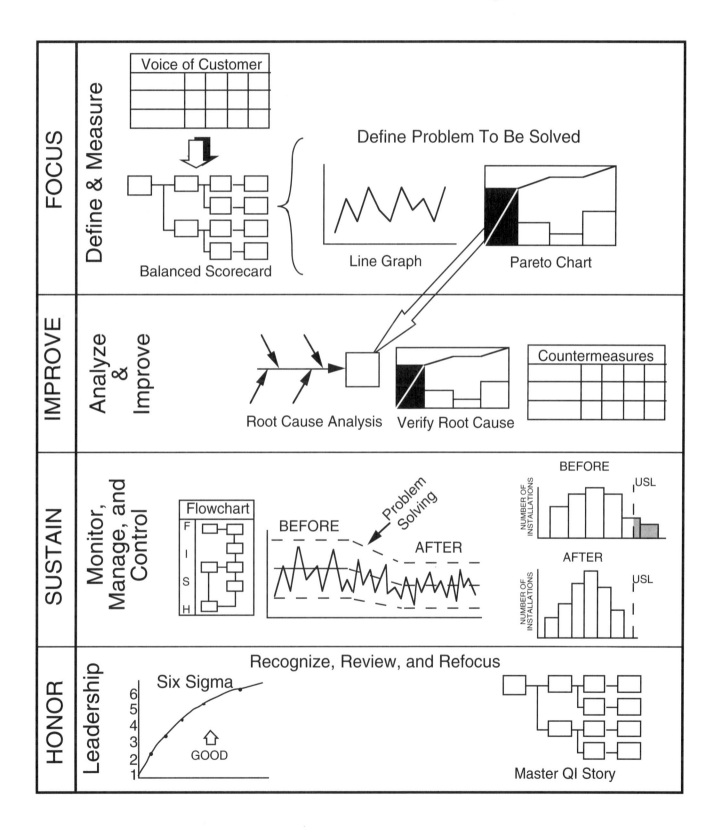

FOCUS — **Define & Measure**

Voice of Customer

Balanced Scorecard

Define Problem To Be Solved

Line Graph

Pareto Chart

IMPROVE — **Analyze & Improve**

Root Cause Analysis — Verify Root Cause — Countermeasures

SUSTAIN — **Monitor, Manage, and Control**

Flowchart

F I S H

BEFORE — Problem Solving — AFTER

BEFORE — NUMBER OF INSTALLATIONS — USL

AFTER — NUMBER OF INSTALLATIONS — USL

HONOR — **Leadership**

Recognize, Review, and Refocus

Six Sigma

6 5 4 3 2 1

GOOD

Master QI Story

Six Sigma Simplified

Step 1: Focus The Improvement

Breakthrough Improvement

Problem:
- It takes too long! We miss commitments!
- Too many defects! Too many customer complaints
- Too much rework and waste! We cost more than our competitors.

Solution: Develop a Balanced Scorecard

Prework: Gather information
- What do our customers really want in terms of:
  - Speed (making and meeting commitments)
  - Quality (low or no defects–outages, errors)
  - Value (i.e., low cost for benefit received)
- What processes deliver the product or service (i.e., value) we provide?
- What measures are already in place?

Develop Laser-Focus

Focused, results-oriented meeting

Purpose: To develop an improvement plan and management system with indicators.

Agenda:
- Analyze customer requirements and pain
- Derive CTQs (i.e., measures) from the customer's requirements
- Develop Balanced Scorecard based on customer requirements, data, and core processes.
- Set BHAG targets for improvement
- Develop initial steps of improvement stories (line graph, pareto chart, problem statement)

Limit: 2 days

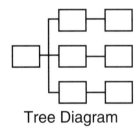

Tree Diagram

Deliverables
- High level customer requirements
- Indicators to measure customer requirements
- Improvement plan with targets to improve key problems

Post Work
- Implement measures
- Initiate problem solving teams to make improvements toward target objectives.
- Review, revise, and refocus indicators and efforts.

Step 2: Improve In Critical Areas

Problem:
- It takes too long! We miss commitments!
- Too many defects! Too many customer complaints
- Too much rework and waste! We cost more than our competitors.

Solution: Focused, Intensive Problem Solving

Prework: Gather information for the meeting
- Performance data:
  - Speed (making and meeting commitments)
  - Quality (low or no defects–outages, errors)
  - Value (i.e., low cost for benefit received)
- Potential root causes

Create Breakthrough Improvements

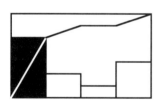
Line Graph

Pareto Chart

Cause-Effect Diagram

Analyze An Element Of The Balanced Scorecard
Purpose: To develop focused improvement stories that will deliver Six Sigma Improvements in speed, quality, and profitability.

Agenda:
- Analyze value-added flow to remove waste and rework.
- Analyze customer pain
- Analyze root causes of problem
- Develop countermeasures and action plan

Limit: 1-2 days

Deliverables
- improvement stories ready for implementation
- Project plan for implementation

Post Work–Results and Standardization
Purpose: To measure results and standardize improvements that will deliver Six Sigma Improvements in speed, quality, and cost.

Agenda:
- Implement countermeasures and track results
- Iterate until targets are achieved.
- Use SPC to monitor and sustain the improvements.

Step 3: Sustain The Improvement

Problem:

- customers want stable, dependable, reliable products and services and we can't provide them 100% of the time.
- problems return after improvement efforts
- unusual circumstances cause problems

Solution: SPC

Prework: Gather information for meeting
- What do our customers really want in terms of:
    - Speed (making and meeting commitments)
    - Quality (low or no defects–outages, errors)
    - Value (i.e., low cost for benefit received)
- What processes deliver the product or service (i.e., value) we provide?
- What are the key areas of customer pain?

Creating A Process Management System

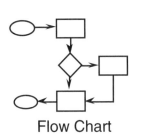
Flow Chart

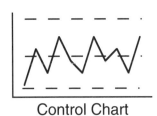
Control Chart

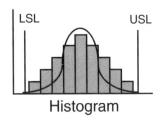
Histogram

Develop a SPC System

Purpose: To identify, document, and stabilize core processes that will deliver the speed, quality, and value our customers crave.

Agenda:
- Flowchart the high-level process and the next lower level
- Develop indicators that will measure and predict your ability to meet customer needs for speed, quality, and cost.
- Develop project plan to implement the process and indicators.

Limit: 2-3 days

Deliverables
- Process documentation–flowcharts
- Indicators to measure process performance
- Project plan for improvement teams

Post Work–Improvement teams

Purpose: To analyze root causes and deliver Six Sigma Improvements in speed, quality, and cost.

Step 4: Train Internal "Belts"

Problem:
- need to train additional employees and solve key problems in a cost effective and timely manner.

Solution: 6σ "Green and BlackBelt" Training

Prework: Experience all aspects of the 6σ process (i.e., serve on successful teams)
- Improvement Focus
  - Speed (making and meeting commitments)
  - Quality (low or no defects–outages, errors)
  - Value (i.e., low cost for benefit received)
- Problem Solving–root cause analysis
- SPC–stabilization

Create Internal Experts

Develop Accelerated Learning And Training Skills
Purpose: To train internal consultants to maximize skill transfer and accelerate organizational success.

Agenda:
- Training flow: Show-Do-Know
- Laser Focus demonstration, elicitation, instructional exercise, and feedback.
- Problem Solving demonstration, elicitation, instructional exercise, and feedback.
- SPC demonstration, elicitation, instructional exercise, and feedback.

Limit: 2 days

Deliverables
- Instructor skills
- Training plans

Post Work–Certification Course
Purpose: To observe instructors presenting in-house course. Recommend areas for improvement. Certify in 6σ methodology.

Agenda:
- Instructors train/facilitate team in 6σ methodology.
- Feedback and areas for improvement
- Certification

Limit: 2 days

Other Processes and Tools

Affinity Diagram

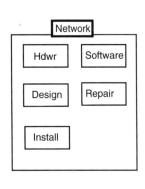

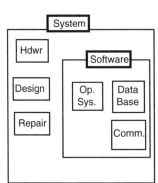

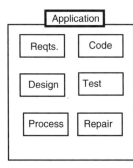

Systems Diagrams

Force Field

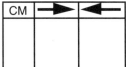

Tree Diagram

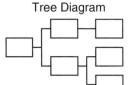

Matrix Diagrams

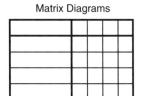

To automate all of your improvement documentation, get *The QI Macros For Microsoft Excel.*
www.qimacros.com/excel-spc.html

Six Sigma Simplified

Tool Definitions

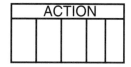

Action Plan: Identify who will do what and when
- What countermeasures to implement
- How to do them
- Who will do them
- When they will be started and completed
- How they will be measured

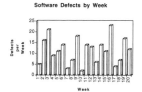

Bar Chart: understand and compare the relative sizes of various data elements. It is an essential part of the Pareto diagram.

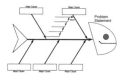

Cause-Effect (Ishikawa) Diagram: Systematically analyze the root causes of problems by asking why, why, why, why, why? It begins with major causes (e.g., process, materials, machines, people, environment) and works backward to root causes.

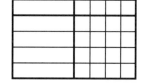

Checksheet: collect small samples of data manually. Checksheets can be in the form of matrices or physical diagrams (e.g., a circuit board and its components).

Control chart: help analyze, sustain, and monitor the current levels of performance stability or predictability of a process and to identify key issues for problem solving or root cause analysis. Control charts have three main elements:
- A center line, usually the average of all of the data points
- An upper control limit (UCL) calculated from the data. (99.7% of all possible points will fall between the upper and the lower control limit.)
- A lower control limit (LCL) calculated from the data.

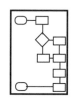

Flow Chart: Show the flow of work through a process including all activities, decisions, and measurement points. There can be macro (high level) and micro (lower level) flowcharts to show increasing layers of detail.

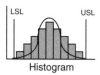

Histogram: Determine the capability (i.e., the level of performance the customers can consistently expect) of the process and the distribution of measurable data.

Line Graph: Show data trends over time. The Y-axis (left) shows the amount of any variable (defects, time, cost) and the X-axis (bottom) shows time (minute, hour, day, week, etc).

         Six Sigma Simplified

Tool Definitions

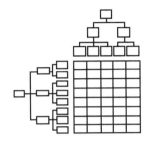

<u>Matrix diagram</u> (e.g., countermeasures or targets and means matrix): Compare two or more groups of ideas, determine relationships among the elements, and make decisions. It helps prioritize tasks or issues to aid decision making and shows linkages between large groups of characteristics, functions, and tasks. Can be combined with tree diagrams.

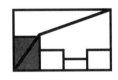

<u>Pareto Chart</u>: Focus the improvement effort by identifying the 20% (vital few) of the contributors that create 80% of the time delay, defects, or costs in any process. The Pareto chart combines a bar graph with a cumulative line graph. The bars are placed from left to right in descending order. The cumulative line graph shows the percent contribution of all preceding bars.

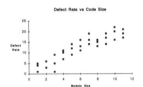

<u>Scatter Diagram</u>: Evaluate the cause-effect relationship, if any, between two variables (e.g., speed and gas consumption in a vehicle). This assists in validating root causes.

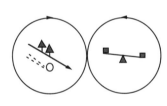

<u>Systems Diagram</u>: Identify cause-effect relationships among related items in a system when the interactions are complex or involved. Unlike the fishbone diagram, the systems diagram can diagnose <u>circular</u> cause-effects in systems. Consists of balancing and reinforcing loops. Each element of the chart is a variable that increases or decreases.

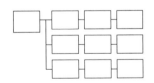

<u>Tree Diagram</u>: Systematically link ideas, targets, objectives, goals, or activities in greater and greater detail. It shows key goals, sub goals, and tasks required to accomplish an objective. It can translate customer desires into product characteristics. It can be used like a cause-effect diagram to uncover root causes. It is a great way to "chunk" and sequence large issues down into smaller, more manageable ones. Can be combined with matrices to prioritize issues.

Affinity Diagram

Affinity Diagram

The affinity diagram helps break old patterns of thought, reveal new patterns, and generate more creative ways of thinking. The affinity diagram helps organize the team's thoughts most effectively when: the issues seem too large and complex; you need to break out of old, traditional ways of thinking; everything seems chaotic; or there are many customer's requirements.

Parts of the overall problem will naturally cluster into components that can be investigated easily. The process is simple:

Affinity Diagram Process

Step	Activity
1.	**State the issue** to be examined in broad terms: "What are the issues surrounding or involving . . . • the delivery of very low defect products or services • reducing cycle time • reducing waste or rework
2.	**Generate and record ideas** using Post-it™ notes. Begin sticking them on a wall or large sheet of easel paper where everyone can see them. Ensure that everyone is included. Ask for a "headline" to describe each thought. Note the contributor's initials.
3.	**Arrange the cards in related groupings.** As you generate ideas, the person at the board may begin grouping the available notes as they are offered and keep the intensity of note generation going as long as possible.
4.	**Complete the groupings.** Involve the group in clustering the notes into 6-10 related groupings. Have everyone stand and do this <u>silently</u>. Be prepared for some "loners." Avoid forcing them into a group. Some notes may need to be duplicated for different groupings.
5.	**Choose a word or phrase that captures the intent of each group** and place it at the top as a header card. If there isn't one already, then create one with a word or phrase that does capture the intent.

Cost of Quality Analysis

Why?

When?

During laser-focus of improvement effort. (Is this problem worth solving?)

How?

1. Identify each step in the Fix-it process.
2. Assign a time in minutes to each task and a loaded rate.
3. Identify any material costs associated with each step.
4. Identify any external costs of this failure.
5. Identify any lost opportunity, asset, or business costs.
6. Set a target for reducing the error (e.g., 50%)
7. Estimate the total cost of achieving this level of prevention.
8. Evaluate ROI.

Evaluate the true costs of a defect or error. This is the foundation of making a business case for the change.

	A	B	C	D	E	F	G
1	Cost of Quality Worksheet						
2	Problem Description: Service Order Errors					Type: Internal	
3	Tasks	Average Hours/ Task	Hourly Rate	Cost of Task	Material Costs	External Failure Cost	Total Cost of Non-Conformance
4	1. Analyze Service Order Error	0.17	$60	$10.00	$3.00	$0.00	$13.00
5	2. Fix Error	0.08	$60	$5.00	$3.00	$0.00	$8.00
6	3. Admin	0.05	$60	$3.00	$0.00	$0.00	$3.00
7	4. Billing Costs Due to Error	0.03	$60	$2.00		$0.00	$2.00
8	Total Cost Per Failure						$26.00
9	Service Order Errors/year						221,000
10	1. Lost Opportunity Costs					$0.00	$0.00
11	2. Lost Assets Costs					$0.00	$0.00
12	3. Lost Business Costs					$0.00	$0.00
13	Additional Failure Costs						$0.00
14	Annual Failure Cost						$5,746,000.00
15						Customer or	
16	Basic tasks to fix the problem	Average min/60	Loaded rate	Calculated cost	Expenses	Employee found	Total
17							
18	Return on Investment and Payback						
19					Target Reduction	50%	$2,873,000
20					Prevention Costs		$225,000
21					ROI		$13:$1
22					Payback Period (days)		17

Types of Costs

Internal Failure Costs:

- Scrap
- Rework
- Failure analysis
- Reinspecting and retesting rework
- Avoidable losses (e.g., overfill)
- Downgrading price due to quality

Appraisal Costs:

- Inspection and test
- Product quality audits
- Measurement system analysis

Prevention Costs:

- Planning
- Statistical Process Control
- Training
- Supplier evaluations

External Failure Costs:

- Warranty Charges
- Complaints and adjustments
- Allowances and concessions

QI Macros Template: costofq.xlt

FMEA
Failure Modes and Effects Analysis

Why?
Recognize and evaluate potential failures of a product or process; Identify actions to prevent the failure; and document the process.

When?
1. New process/ design
2. Modified process/ design
3. Existing process applied in new environment

How?
1. Enter part name
2. List each potential failure mode
3. Describes effects of each type of failure
4. Rank severity of failure
5. Classify any special characteristics
6. List every potential cause or failure mechanism for each failure mode.
7. Estimate the likelihood of occurrence of each failure/cause
8. List prevention/ detection controls
9. Rank detection
10. Identify actions to reduce severity, occurrence, and detection.

Failure Mode and Effects Analysis									AIAG Third Edition				
System:		Design Responsibility:			FMEA Number								
Subsystem		Key Date:	1/1/03		Page	1	of	1					
Component					Prepared by:								
Model:					FMEA Date:	1/1/03							
Core Team:										Action Results			

Severity of Effect:
1. None
2. Very Minor
3. Minor
4. Very Low
5. Low
6. Moderate
7. High
8. Very High
9. Hazardous with warning
10. Hazardous w/o warning

Occurrence Ratin:
1. Remote <.01/1000
2. Low -0.1/1000
3. Low -0.5/1000
4. Moderate - 1/1000
5. Moderate - 2/1000
6. Moderate -5/1000
7. High - 10/1000
8. High - 20/1000
9. Very High 50/1000
10. Very High >100/1

Detection:
1. Almost Certain
2. Very High
3. High
4. Moderate High
5. Moderate
6. Low
7. Very Low
8. Remote
9. Very Remote
10. Absolute Uncer

Detection:
1. Almost Certain
2. Very High
3. High
4. Moderate High
5. Moderate
6. Low
7. Very Low
8. Remote
9. Very Remote
10. Absolute Uncertainty

RPN= RISK Priority Number

Sample

Failure Mode and Effects Analysis									AIAG Third Edition				
System:		Design Responsibility:			FMEA Number								
Subsystem		Key Date:	1/1/03		Page	1	of	1					
Component					Prepared by:								
Model:					FMEA Date:	1/1/03							
Core Team:										Action Results			

Item/Part Function	Potential Failure Mode	Potential Effect(s) of Failure	Sev	Cl	Potential Cause(s)/Mechanism(s) of Failure	Occ	Current Design Controls Prevention	Current Design Controls Detection	Det	R.P.N.	Recommended Action(s)	Responsibility & Target Completion Date	Actions Taken	Sev	Occ	Det	R.P.N.
Front Door LH	Corroded interior lower door Panels	Deteriorated life of door leading to	7		Upper edge of protective wax application specified for inner door panels is too low	6		Vehicle general durability test	7	294	Add Laboratory accelerated corrosion testing	A Tate-Body Engineering Corrosion testing	Based on test results, upper edge spec raised 125mm	7	2	2	28
		1. Unsatisfactory appearance due to rust through paint over time	7		Insufficient wax thickness specified	4		Vehicle general durability test	7	196	Conduct DOE on wax thickness	A.Tate	Thickness is adequate	7	2	2	28
		2. Impaired function of interior door hardware	7		Insufficient room between panels for spray head access	4		Drawing evaluation of spray head access	4	112	Add team evaluation using design aid buck and spray head	Body Engineering	Evaluation showed adequate access	7	1	1	7

QI Macros Template: FMEA.xlt

Force Field Analysis

Purpose

Identify the potential roadblocks and problems associated with implementing a countermeasure

Progress is a nice word. But change is its motivator. And change has its enemies.
 - Robert F. Kennedy

Even though there are good reasons for eliminating the weeds in any garden, there will always be barriers to improvement. Well implemented countermeasures anticipate and prevent these barriers.

Force Field Analysis

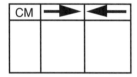

CM	➤	◄

1. Brainstorm the <u>existing</u> forces acting against the introduction of a countermeasure–resources (time and money), existing ways of doing things.

2. Brainstorm the <u>existing</u> forces that can help overcome these barriers. Match them to the barriers.

3. Identify the forces acting against implementation that still require action.

4. Use them to help develop the action plan.

Force Field Analysis

Counter measures	Forces	
	For	Against
	QI Macros Template: forcefld.xlt	

Matrix Diagram

Matrix Diagrams

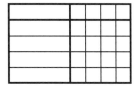

Matrix Diagrams

(Example, page 39.)

The matrix diagram helps prioritize tasks or issues in ways that aid decision making; identify the connecting points between large groups of characteristics, functions, and tasks; or show the ranking or priority of in an interaction.

Combined with tree diagrams, prioritization matrices can rank various choices in terms of impact on the customer, reduction in cycle time, defects, costs, and so on.

Matrices can be used in many ways to show relationships. They can be shaped like an L, a T, an X, or a three-dimensional, inverted Y. The L-shaped matrix helps display relationships among any two different groups of people, processes, materials, machines, or environmental factors. The T-shaped diagram is simply two L-shaped diagrams connected together showing the relationships of two different factors to a common third one. The Y-shaped matrix helps identify interactions among three different factors. The X-shaped matrix (two T's back to back) is occasionally useful.

QFD House of Quality

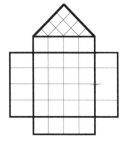
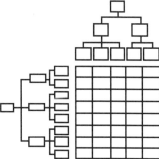
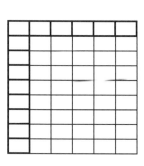
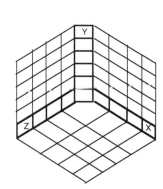

Matrix Process

Step	Activity
1.	**Generate two or more sets of characteristics** to be compared. Use tree diagrams or brainstorming.
2.	**Choose the proper matrix** to represent the interactions (L, T, X, Y).
3.	**Put the characteristics on the axes** of the matrix.
4.	**Rank the interactions** from 1 (low) to 5 (high).

     Six Sigma Simplified

SIPOC

Purpose   Identify the suppliers, inputs, process, outputs and customers of any process.

S	I	P	O	C
Suppliers	**Inputs**	**Process**	**Outputs**	**Customers**
Provider	Input requirements and measures	Start:	Output requirements and measures	Receiver
		High-Level Process Description		
		End:		

1. Describe the process and start/end points.
2. Identify customers of your process.
3. Identify process outputs
4. Identify process inputs.
5. Identify suppliers to your process.

QI Macros Template: SIPOC.xlt

Systems Diagrams

Systems Diagram Symbols

Systems Diagram

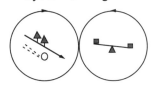

It is best to do things systematically, since we are only human, and disorder is our worst enemy.
  -Hesiod

The systems diagram helps map the logical relationships between the related items. The systems diagram shows the cause-effect relationships among many key elements. It can be used to identify the causes of problems or to work backward from a desired outcome to identify all of the causal factors that would need to exist to ensure the achievement of an outcome. A systems diagram uses a few simple symbols to show the circular cause-effects in a system. The symbols are:

	Indicator	Measures the effect of some force in the system (amount or number of ...)
	Arrow	Showing the cause-effects among indicators.
	Delay	Lag between cause and effect
S or O	Same/Opposite	Cause Effect relationship

Systems Diagram Process

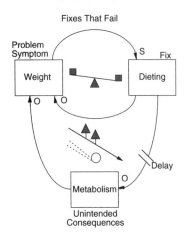

Step	Activity
1.	**State the system, problem or issue** under discussion
2.	**Generate cause-effect issues** by brainstorming things that are either increasing or decreasing.
3.	**Draw <u>one-way</u> arrows to indicate the cause-effect relationship** among the components of the diagram.
4.	**Identify the effects.** If the an *increase* in A causes an increase in B, then put the letter "S" on the arrow. If an *increase* in A causes a *decrease* in B, then put the letter "O" on the arrow near B.

QI Macros Template: relation.xlt

Tree Diagram

Tree Diagram

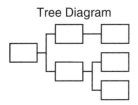

The tree diagram can map specific tasks to primary and secondary goals. It maps the methods required to achieve corporate goals. The tree diagram shows the key goals, their sub-goals, and key tasks. It can help identify the sequence of tasks or functions required to accomplish an objective. The tree diagram can help translate customer desires into product characteristics. It can also be used like an Ishikawa diagram to uncover the causes of a particular problem.

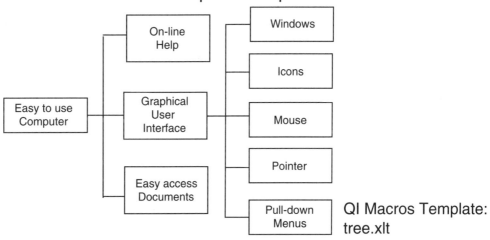

QI Macros Template: tree.xlt

Tree Diagram Process

The process for constructing the tree diagram is similar to the Ishikawa diagram in many respects:

Step	Activity
1.	**Develop a clear statement of the problem**, issue, or objective to be addressed. Place it on the left side of a board, wall, or easel and work toward the right.
2.	**Brainstorm all of the sub-goals, tasks, or criteria** necessary to accomplish or resolve the issue.
3.	**Repeat this process** using each of the sub-goals until only actionable tasks or elements remain.
4.	**Check the logic of the diagram** in the same way as the Ishikawa: Start at the right and work your way back to the left by asking: "If we do this, will it lead to the accomplishment of the previous task?"

Affordable SPC Power Tools for Six Sigma

If you're moving up to Six Sigma, the new ISO standard, or the standards set by JCAHO (hospital quality), you need a fast, easy, and affordable way to do all of your control charts, capability studies, and improvement documentation using data that's probably already in Microsoft Excel.

Excel by itself won't draw paretos, histograms, or control charts. But with the QI Macros (add-in macros and templates for Excel), line, pie, bar, pareto, histogram, scatter, and control charts are just a mouse click away. All you have to do is select the data you want graphed and, in just seconds, the macro will ***do all the math and draw the graph*** for you. It's perfect for line employees. Even if you have a more expensive SPC package, the QI Macros eliminate the need to import the data from Excel or Access! The package includes over 40 fill-in-the-blanks templates for QFD, DOE, Gage R&R, Cause-Effect, and many other common tools. So why waste your valuable time learning new software when you can just use Excel and the QI Macros?

Consider how simple it can be to create a Pareto Chart:

1. From your Excel worksheet (right), *select the data* to be graphed:

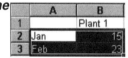

	A	B
1		Plant 1
2	Jan	15
3	Feb	23

2. Click on the QI Macros pull-down menu in Excel (right). ***Select Pareto Chart.*** The QI macro will do the math and draw the graph (below). It's easy!

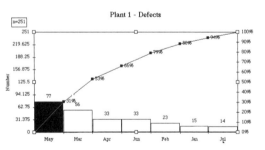

Plant 1 - Defects

QI Macros	
Line Graph	Ctrl+Shift+L
Pareto Chart	Ctrl+Shift+M
Bar Graph	Ctrl+Shift+B
Pie Chart	Ctrl+Shift+O
Scatter Diagram	Ctrl+Shift+S
Frequency	Ctrl+Shift+F
Histogram	Ctrl+Shift+H
XmR, XRs Chart	Ctrl+Shift+R
XmR, XRs Trend	Ctrl+Shift+T
XbarR Chart	Ctrl+Shift+X
c Chart	Ctrl+Shift+C
np Chart	Ctrl+Shift+N
p Chart	Ctrl+Shift+P
u Chart	Ctrl+Shift+U
Control Chart Selector	
Matrix and Diagram Selector	

The Pareto Chart ***alone*** is worth it. Then, ***unlike*** other statistics packages, the QI templates automate most other common QI forms and tools—flowcharts, Ishikawa diagrams, and matrices—even QFD House of Quality. ***Start automating your graphs and improvement stories today!***

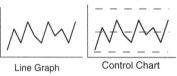
Line Graph   Control Chart

Pareto Chart

Histogram

Cause-Effect Diagram

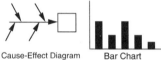
Bar Chart

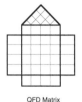
QFD Matrix

Pie Chart

Flow Chart

Scatter Diagram

Tree Diagram

1) You Can: DMAIC Any Process With The QI Macros

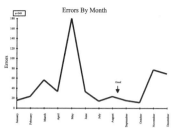
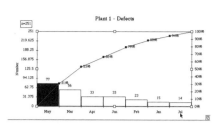
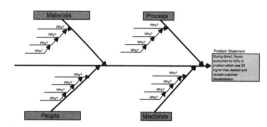

2) Control the Process with Flow Charts, SPC, Control Charts, Histograms, and Capability Studies

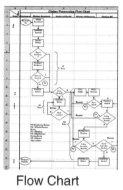
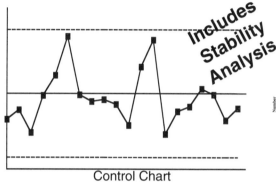
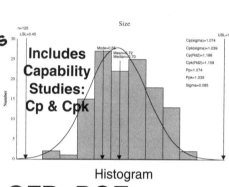

Flow Chart   Control Chart   Histogram

3) DFSS (Design For Six Sigma), QFD, DOE—Design of Experiments, and MSA—GageR&R

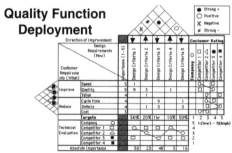
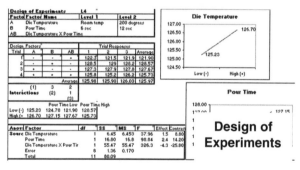

4) ANOVA, Regression, and Hypothesis Testing

You Get All of These Charts for only $129!		Plus 35 "Fill-in-the-blanks" Templates		Statistical Tools
■ XbarR Chart	■ c Chart	Action Plan	Force Field Analysis	Anova: Single Factor
■ XandS Chart	■ u Chart	Affinity	**Gage R&R** Matrix	Anova: Two Factor
■ XmR (Individuals) Chart	■ np Chart	Arrow	**Ishikawa** Diagram	Correlation
■ XmR Trend	■ p Chart	Block	L-, T-, X-shaped Matrices	Covariance
■ Histogram with Cp, Cpk	■ Frequency Histogram	Checksheet	PDPC Chart	Exponential Smoothing
■ Box & Whisker Chart	■ Multivari Chart	Countermeasures Matrix	Pugh Concept Selection	F-Test: Two-sample
■ Line, Run, Bar, Pie Charts	■ Cusum Chart	Cost-of-Quality Analysis	**QFD** House of Quality	Moving Average
■ Pareto Chart	■ Scatter Diagram	Cost-Benefit Analysis	Relationship Diagram	Rank and Percentile
		Design of Experiments	Targets and Means	Regression
		EMEA/FMEA	Transition Planning	t-Test: Two Factor
		Fault Tree	**Tree** Diagram	z-Test: Two-sample
		Flow Chart	Voice of the Customer	

Actual QI Macros Graphs and Templates

QI Macros - Quantity Discounts

Get "seats" for all of the users that need the QI Macros.

36 pg. User Guide + CD-ROM

You can get five copies of the QI Macros and still spend less than you would for one copy of most other brands of SPC software.

Quantity Discounts

Quantity	Price:	S&H
2-4 copies	$119	$8+$2/copy
5-49 Licenses:	$99	$8+$2/copy
50-99 Licenses	$89	$50
100-249 Licenses:	$79	$75

QI Macros - Site Licensing

Total PCs	Price/ copy	Discount	Total Cost Per Seat Price	Enterprise License
250-374	$69	46%	$17,250-$25,000	$15,995
375-499	$69	46%	Up to $34,500	$24,995
500-749	$69	46%	Up to $51,500	$34,995
750-999	$69	46%	Up to $69,000	$49,995
1000-2499	$59	54%	Up to $147,000	$59,995
2500-5000	$49	62%	Up to $245,000	$99,995

Price Comparison

For this many copies of Minitab	Price	You could get this many copies of the QI Macros
1	$1,195	12 @ $99
25	$22,375	450
50	$39.750	800
100	$69,500	2,600

Customer Comments

We hit 420 days without a lost time accident while in Chapter 11, and that was a savings of $750,000 in lost time accidents from the year before. One of the tools I used to make this happen was QI Macros with the Training CD. **—Richard Borcicky**

The QI Macros save our clients an estimated 75% of their documentation time and cost. **– Joe Farina - PerformTech**

The QI Macros are just common sense — which I consider the 'new brilliance. **– James Espinosa, MD**

Yes! I want Jay Arthur's fast, fun and easy-to-use Six Sigma Simplified System to work for me! *Please send the software and training material indicated.* (Offer good until 12/

☐ **Green Belt System:** (#290)	☐ **Team Leader System:** (#260)	☐ **Six Sigma Starter Kit:** (# 255)
QI Macros (#230) +Training CD (#237)	QI Macros (#230)	QI Macros (#230)
70 pg. Six Sigma Tools (#239)	Training CD (#237)	Training CD (#237)
192 pg. Instructor Guide (#210)	*70 pg. Six Sigma Tools (#239)*	*70 pg. Six Sigma Tools (#239)*
128 pg. Six Sigma Simplified (#205)	*128 pg. Six Sigma Simplified (#205)*	*128 pg. Six Sigma Simplified (#205)*
Video (#265, 267/8) & Audio (#225)	*192 pg. Instructor Guide (#210)*	
☐ DVD ☐ VHS ☐ Mfg ☐ Health		
Only $499.95 Save $50	**Only $209.95** Save $37	**Only $179.95** Save $27
includes $15 S&H, **add** *$25 for FedEx*	*includes $10 S&H,* **add** *$25 for FedEx*	*includes $10 S&H,* **add** *$25 for FedEx*

Qty.	Item	Order Form	Price	FedEx	3-Day Mail	Item Total
	230	QI Macros for Excel (discounts for 2 or more, see page 3)	$129.00	$20	$8	
	237	QI Macros Training CD ROM	$19.95	$20	$8	
	239	Six Sigma Tools (Example Book)	$19.95	$20	$8	
	205	Six Sigma Simplified Team Member Workbook	$29.95	$20	$8	
	210	Six Sigma Instructor Guide–Greenbelt Training Made Easy	$39.95	$20	$8	
	220	Small Business Guerrilla Guide to Six Sigma	$9.95	$20	$8	
	225	Six Sigma Simplified (4-Audiotapes & Training Guide)	$49.95	$20	$8	
	265	Six Sigma Green Belt (☐ DVD ☐ VHS & Training Guide)	$199.95	$20	$8	
	267	SPC Simplified Video (☐ DVD ☐ VHS) (☐ Mfg ☐ Health)	$99.00	$20	$8	
Shipping and Handling:		**First individual item: $8 (Mail) or $20 (FedEx)**				
		Each additional Item: $2 (Mail) or $5 (FedEx)				
					Order Total	

Please type or print clearly or attach business card here

Company _____

Your Name _____

Mailing Address_____

P.O. Box _____ Apt/Ste. _____

City, ST, Zip _____

Phone _____

Fax _____

Email _____

☐ Check here if you have ordered from us before

Yes! We also accept Purchase Orders!

Purchase Order Number _____
(to prevent duplicate shipments, <u>never</u> send confirming POs)

☐ VISA ☐ MasterCard ☐ AMEX
_____ Exp._____

Signature_____

☐ I've enclosed my check, VISA, MasterCard, or AmEx.

☐ I want to try them out **Absolutely Risk Free**. Please send my order immediately. *I have 30 days to pay the invoice or return them with no obligation.*

Order by 4/30/2004 to Receive these Special Bonuses
Special Bonus #1 - *Small Biz Guerrilla Guide to Six Sigma*
Special Bonus #2 - *Six Sigma Quick Reference Cards*

Orders Only
(To minimize errors please order online or fax your order)

Order Online at: **www.sixsigmatoolbelt.com**

FAX your order toll-free to: **(888) 468-1536** or
(303) 753-9675

Mail to: LifeStar, 2244 S. Olive St. Denver, CO 80224

Orders-only, Call Toll-free: (888) 468-1535 or
(Please have your item # ready) (303) 757-2039

Questions about the QI Macros?
email: lifestar@rmi.net, knowwareman@qimacros.com
9a.m. and 5p.m. MST   **(888) 468-1537** or
(303) 756-9144

LifeStar

Jay Arthur
2244 S. Olive St.
Denver, CO 80224
TEL (888) 468-1537
　　　(303) 756-9144
FAX (888) 468-1536
　　　(303) 756-3107
lifestar@rmi.net
www.qimacros.com

Upgrade Your KnowWare®!

Tree Diagram

Line Graph

Pareto Chart

Cause-Effect Diagram

Flow Chart

Control Chart

Need Help With Your First Project?

Breakthrough Improvement Made Easy

Problem:
- Need Breakthrough Improvement

Solution: Jump Start Your Results

Develop understanding of Six Sigma and apply it
Purpose: To complete a project that saves $250,000+.
Agenda:

- Focus on 4% that will give 50% of return (3 days)
    - Speed (making and meeting commitments)
    - Quality (low or no defects--outages, errors)
    - Value (i.e., low cost for benefit received)

- Improve–root cause analysis (3 to 5 teams, 1 day each)
    - Line–to determine trends
    - Pareto–to find 4% causing 50% of waste & rework
    - Fishbone–to analyze root causes
    - Countermeasures matrix–to identify solutions
    - Action plan–to implement improvements

- Sustain–SPC (2 days)
    - Flow Charts–to define and refine the process
    - Control Charts–choosing the right chart
        - X charts for time, weight, length
        - Attribute charts for defects, failures
    - Histograms–to analyze capability

Limit: 10 days, $50,000

Deliverables
- Breakthrough improvements worth $250,000
- Awareness and understanding of Six Sigma

Jay Arthur works with operational managers faced with rising costs and shrinking budgets who want to boost productivity and profitability. You can spend up to nine months and an estimated $250,000 to develop just one blackbelt. Doesn't it make sense to start improving the bottom line while you find out who has the right mindset to lead your Six Sigma efforts? To find out more, visit our website: www.qimacros.com

---